LIVING LONGER HEALTHIER AND HAPPIER

YOUR CLEAR PATH TO AGELESS VITALITY

By

Fiona Kable

Fiona Kable

Contents

INTRODUCTION

The Quest For Eternal Vitality: Embracing The Journey To A Healthier, Happier, And Longer Life

"I am beautiful, one with cosmos, life force, eternal."
- Jay Woodman

Jay Woodman's affirmation shines a beacon on the beauty of living life to its fullest. It's a gentle reminder of the extraordinary potential nestled within you; a treasure often left undiscovered in the rush of city life. Technology and urban sprawl were welcomed with open arms because they promised to make everything simpler, to keep us connected. Yet, somehow, they've nudged us away from the natural world, from a deeper understanding of ourselves, and from the simple joys that make life truly vibrant. In this pursuit of ease, we're actually caught in a tangle of health challenges, witnessing the earth suffer and feeling a disconnect that's hard to explain. It's a paradox, isn't it? In trying to enrich our lives, it seems we've traded in the very essence that makes them worth living.

I see you. You, carrying the days on your shoulders, not as medals of experience but as chains of weariness. You, starting your mornings already exhausted, drifting through your days in a haze, lying in bed at night pondering the depth of your existence. The aches, the relentless tiredness, the feeling of being alone in a crowd — these aren't just personal battles. They're signs of a collective drift from what matters most.

I see you, looking for clarity in a sea of complex health tips and fleeting diet trends that promise the moon but leave you in the dark. It might feel as if the keys to wellness are locked behind a door to which only a select few have access. But let me reassure you, the journey to rediscovering your vitality and joy isn't out of reach. It doesn't lie in the elusive or the complicated. It's about peeling back the layers to find the simplicity and truth at the core of your being. Your quest for answers, your desire for a life filled with energy and peace, has brought you here. And I'm here to tell you, you're not navigating this path alone. We're collectively looking to build a life that's not just lived but cherished, every single day.

What if I told you that the secret to a vibrant, joyous, and long life is already in your hands? This book is your treasure map, guiding you toward the heart of living well. It advocates for easy, lasting modifications that profoundly impact your life. Within its chapters, you'll uncover the overlooked shortcuts to vitality, hidden by the hustle of our times. These aren't quick, ephemeral fixes but deeply rooted truths, backed by science and proven by practice, crafted into actionable steps for your everyday life. This book offers a holistic roadmap to well-being and vitality, drawing inspiration from the longevity secrets of the Blue Zones and cutting-edge biohacking techniques to unlock your body's full potential.

You'll be learning to leverage sleep as a tool for mental and physical renewal, turning meals into a defense against illness while keeping your energy levels high, and fostering a mindset that nurtures longevity and happiness. These are the pathways to a life not merely endured but richly enjoyed. Imagine greeting each new day charged with enthusiasm, navigating your daily adventures with a clear, focused purpose that once felt beyond reach.

This pursuit of well-being isn't just for you; it's a gift you'll pass on to the coming generations. Our decisions have far-reaching effects, touching the lives of those around us and the health of our planet. We're all woven into life's vast tapestry, our lives intertwined and mutually dependent.

As you begin reading the book, see it not merely as advice but as a companion on your path to lasting health and vigor. This journey is a perpetual discovery of living in sync with ourselves and our environment. If you've ever felt adrift in a sea of conflicting health tips, if you've yearned for a deeper sense of vitality and joy, take heart: you've found your haven. This isn't just another biohacking book; it's a declaration for a refreshed approach to life, inspiring you to regain your well-being, happiness, and longevity through simple, enduring shifts. So let's get to it!

Author's Note

I am Fiona Kable, a quantum transformational coach whose career was shaped by personal adversity. After facing significant stress and overwhelm, I found my way to healing and empowerment. This journey sharpened my skills in guiding others through their transformative paths toward growth and self-discovery.

My purpose emerged from the need to conquer life's challenging storms, and this deep personal transformation anchors my coaching philosophy. I now embody the strength that springs from vulnerability and the possibility of renewal through self-care and introspection.

This book, 'Living Longer, Healthier and Happier: Your Clear Path to Ageless Vitality,' represents my approach to wellness and longevity. It goes beyond conventional advice, offering strategies grounded in mindful practices and spiritual balance.

My commitment to building community, fostering connections, and providing compassionate coaching is the foundation of my work. Through my writings and coaching, I aim to ignite the inner spirit of my readers and clients, helping them lead lives that are not only healthier but also more enriched and satisfying. For more insights into Lumina Transformational

Coaching, visit www.luminatransformationalcoaching.com or @lumina_transformation

CHAPTER 1

Unveiling The Secrets Of Longevity

"Step back in time and do something youthful, and your biology will mirror that."

-*Cari Corbet Owen*

This intriguing thought, shared by Cari Corbet Owen, offers a glimpse into the truth about the essence of longevity. It's a concept that goes beyond the mere ticking of our biological clocks or the accumulation of years. At its core, longevity is about the quality of those years, filled with vitality, health, and happiness. It invites us to challenge the conventional boundaries of aging, to rediscover the youthful spirit within, and to reflect that vitality in our physical being. But what does longevity truly mean? Is it a quest for the fabled fountain of youth, an impossible dream of immortality? Or is there a scientific foundation for the idea that we can live longer, healthier lives? This chapter dives deep into the heart of these questions, exploring the science behind aging well and separating the myths from the realities.

Aging is an inevitable part of life, yet how we age is profoundly influenced by our lifestyle choices, environmental factors, and even our mindset.

Scientific research has begun to unravel the complex mechanisms that govern our biological aging process, offering insights into how we can potentially slow down this process and, more importantly, improve our health span—the period of life spent in good health. As we explore the myths and realities surrounding longevity, we'll examine how modern science supports ancient wisdom and how, sometimes, what we believe to be true about aging is more fiction than fact. From the idea that genetics solely determine our lifespan to the belief that aging must inevitably bring decline, I'll uncover the truths that will empower you to take control of your aging process.

Understanding Longevity: Demystifying the Science Behind Aging Well

The idea of longevity can lead to thoughts about achieving immortality, similar to stories of magical potions or futuristic scientific discoveries. But what truly lies at the heart of longevity? It's not about chasing after an unattainable dream of living forever; it's about enriching longevity with quality and zest, aiming to live longer and better.

The intricacies of aging involve a delicate balance between genetics, our daily choices, and the environment around us. Studies highlight that although genetics play a key role, the decisions we make each day significantly influence how gracefully we age. From a scientific standpoint, aging is marked by a slow decline in cellular and overall body functions. Yet, this doesn't have to mean an unavoidable slide into illness and frailty. Rather, it's a journey that can be steered positively by how we choose to live.

Several myths persist regarding the aging process and the determinants of longevity. One widespread belief is that our lifespan is locked in by our genetic code, leaving us little room to make an impact. According to the Danish Twin Study, our genes only influence about 20% of our lifespan. The other 80% is all about the choices we make (Herskind et al., 1996)! While genetics set some boundaries, epigenetic advancements reveal that our lifestyle and environment can profoundly affect gene expression (Kanherkar, Bhatia-Dey, & Csoka, 2014). This insight opens up the possibility that adopting healthy habits can not only lengthen our lives but also enhance their quality.

It's also a myth that longevity requires extreme diets or intense exercise routines. Research indicates that simple, sustainable lifestyle changes can offer substantial longevity benefits. Take the Mediterranean diet as an example: its emphasis on fruits, vegetables, and healthy fats is associated with lower heart disease risks and a longer life (Estruch et al., 2013). True longevity is achieved through a holistic strategy that balances nutrition, physical activity, mental stimulation, and social engagement. It's about taking care of both body and mind in ways that support our well-being at every stage of life.

By understanding the science of aging, you can empower yourself to make choices that transform your approach to growing older. Stop dreading getting older and start celebrating each year. This makes us want to live healthier, not just for longer, but for a happier and more fulfilling life.

Discovering Blue Zones: Lessons from the World's Oldest Living Populations

Blue Zones are intriguing spots on the map where people enjoy remarkably longer lives than the global average. These regions, highlighted by Dan Buettner's work with National Geographic, are home to an impressive number of centenarians—individuals who reach or surpass 100 years of life. Notable Blue Zones include Sardinia in Italy, Okinawa in Japan, Loma Linda in California, Nicoya in Costa Rica, and Ikaria in Greece.

The magic of these areas lies not in their scenic beauty or climate but in their residents' lifestyles. These communities share lifestyle habits that significantly contribute to longevity (Buettner & Skemp, 2016).

Blue Zones' Lifestyle Principles

The core principles found in Blue Zones blend nutrition, physical activity, social involvement, and a sense of purpose. These aren't about radical life overhauls or intense exercise regimens but about weaving straightforward, enduring habits into your everyday routine. This includes adopting a plant-centric diet, participating in regular, gentle physical activities like walking or gardening, valuing family and community ties, and nurturing a sense of belonging and purpose in life (Buettner & Skemp, 2016).

Embrace Movement in Daily Life: The secret behind the vitality of the world's oldest folks isn't found in gym memberships or intense workout sessions but in weaving natural motion into the fabric of their everyday activities. Whether it's a stroll around the neighborhood, tending to a garden, or simply doing chores around the house, these gentle, regular movements play a pivotal role.

Find Your Purpose: In places like Okinawa and Nicoya, having a clear sense of purpose—or "Ikigai" and "Plan de Vida," respectively—can add up to seven years to your life expectancy. It's about knowing you have something valuable to contribute, giving you a compelling reason to greet each day.

Learn to Unwind: In a world where stress is a constant, those who live longest know the importance of letting go. Whether through meditation, prayer, napping, or enjoying a leisurely happy hour, finding ways to decompress is crucial for warding off the chronic inflammation linked with age-related diseases.

Eat Mindfully: The practice of "Hara Hachi Bu," an ancient mantra reminding Okinawans to stop eating when 80% full, underscores the importance of eating until you're just satisfied, not stuffed. This mindful eating can be a key factor in maintaining a healthy weight.

Prefer Plants: In the diets of those who reach 100 and beyond, beans—like fava, black, soy, and lentils—are the main attraction. Meat is enjoyed sparingly, highlighting a diet rich in plant-based nutrients.

Enjoy Wine Wisely: Regular, moderate consumption of wine, shared with friends or over a meal, is a common thread in Blue

Zones, save for Adventists. This isn't about indulging all at once but enjoying a glass or two dailies to enhance longevity.

Foster Connections: Nearly all centenarians belong to a faith community, showing that the fellowship offered by regular spiritual gatherings can extend life by 4-14 years, regardless of the denomination.

Put Family First: Centenarians make their family a priority, often keeping elderly relatives close or within their homes, committing deeply to partners, and nurturing their children with time and affection. This family-first approach has profound implications for health and longevity.

Choose Your Circle Wisely: Long-lived individuals often find themselves in or actively choose social circles that promote healthy living. The concept of "moais" in Okinawa—lifelong commitment groups of friends—exemplifies how surrounding yourself with those supporting positive health behaviors can significantly influence your own habits.

Integrating Blue Zones principles into your life can benefit your health and happiness. It doesn't mean you have to move to these areas; rather, it's about infusing their lifestyle habits into your own life, wherever you may be. This might involve tweaking your diet to be more plant-forward, seeking natural ways to stay active throughout the day, dedicating effort to deepen connections with loved ones, and finding what deeply motivates you (Buettner, 2009).

Distinguishing Between Myths and Truths Pertaining to Blue Zones

While Blue Zones captivate many with their promise of extended life, it's vital to discern the myths from the truths. The myth suggests a secret formula exclusive to these areas. However, the truth reveals that longevity principles are attainable by anyone, anywhere. It boils down to lifestyle choices that are adaptable by people globally, independent of their location.

Learning from the world's longest-lived individuals shows us that the keys to a long, satisfying life are closer than we might think. Consciously aligning our daily choices with the habits seen in these extraordinary communities can go a long way. By doing so, you can "turn back the clock," in a manner of speaking, to display youthfulness, vigor, and, ultimately, a longer life that reflects the essence of Blue Zones (Buettner, 2009).

Myth: Blue Zones Are Mystical or Exclusive Retreats

Truth: Let me clear the air – Blue Zones aren't shrouded in mystery or reserved for a select few. They've been spotlighted through diligent research for their unique lifestyle and community habits that fuel extraordinary life spans. From the serene hills of Ikaria, Greece, to the vibrant shores of Okinawa, Japan, these remarkable places like Sardinia, Italy, Nicoya, Costa Rica, and Loma Linda, California, open their secrets to all. Blue Zones' magic lies in their people's life-enriching practices rather than any hidden geographical charm (Buettner, 2009).

Myth: Longevity Is Mostly In Your Genes

Truth: While it's true that genes get a say in how long you'll live, your lifestyle and surroundings sing the louder chorus. Investigations into Blue Zones have unveiled that how you live your life – your eating habits, your daily movement, and how you connect with others – plays a starring role in your journey to a ripe old age, often dimming the spotlight on genetic factors (Buettner & Skemp, 2016).

Myth: Diets from Blue Zones Are Complicated and Hard to Mimic

Truth: There's nothing overly intricate or strict about the diets from Blue Zones. These dietary patterns prioritize a simplified approach, emphasizing whole, unrefined grains, a variety of plant-based foods, legumes, nuts, and occasional fish or meat. This focus on nutrient-rich, unprocessed foods fosters both wholesomeness and accessibility for most people (Buettner & Skemp, 2016).

Biohacking Your Way to Health: Sleep & Fasting

In the journey toward a life filled with vitality and longevity, I've come across two time-honored practices that modern science has begun to shine a light on: the art of mastering sleep and the discipline of intermittent fasting. These practices, rooted deeply in the tapestry of human history, are making a powerful comeback, spotlighting the intrinsic wisdom of our ancestors through the lens of today's biohacking culture. While these methods might seem simple at first glance, they offer a deep dive into the intricate dance of our body's natural rhythms and needs.

Mastering Sleep: A Timeless Voyage

The power of sleep has been celebrated through the ages, from ancient civilizations that built temples for dream-induced healing to today's world, where the quest for productivity often leaves our need for rest in the shadows. This neglect has led to a silent epidemic of sleep deprivation, silently chipping away at our health and our years.

Yet, there's hope on the horizon. The explosion of sleep science has rekindled our fascination with the night's rest, revealing its essential role in everything from consolidating memories to regulating emotions and maintaining metabolic health. Figures like William C. Dement and Michel Jouvet have mapped the landscapes of sleep, showing us that

Optimizing our sleep is not merely about dodging disorders but about elevating our daily functioning, mood, and even extending our lifespan.

Sleep Optimization Techniques

1. Establish a Consistent Sleep Schedule

Your body thrives on routine. Aim to go to bed and wake up at the same time every day, even on weekends. This regularity reinforces your body's sleep-wake cycle, enhancing sleep quality (Hirshkowitz et al., 2015).

2. Create a Restful Environment

Minimize noise, light, and electronic distractions in your bedroom. Consider blackout curtains, white noise machines, and keeping devices out of the bedroom to promote uninterrupted sleep (Boyce et al., 2016).

3. Limit Exposure to Blue Light

Exposure to blue light from screens can disrupt your circadian rhythm. Reduce screen time at least an hour before bed or use blue light filtering apps and glasses (Chang et al., 2015).

4. Embrace a Pre-Sleep Routine

Engage in calming activities before bed, such as reading, meditation, or a warm bath. These can help signal to your body that it's time to wind down (Black et al., 2015).

5. Mind Your Intake

Avoid caffeine and heavy meals close to bedtime. Both can disrupt sleep patterns, delaying sleep onset and affecting sleep quality (Drake et al., 2013).

Intermittent Fasting: A Tradition Reborn

Intermittent fasting is a practice as ancient as time itself, woven into the fabric of various religious and cultural traditions. These rituals were not just spiritual exercises but were also grounded in an intuitive understanding of fasting's benefits for both body and spirit—insights that are now echoed by scientific research.

Central to the scientific discourse on intermittent fasting is the understanding that periods of fasting afford the body a necessary respite from the continual process of digestion. This pause allows the body's energy to be reallocated towards cellular repair and regeneration (de Cabo & Mattson, 2019). Moreover, fasting initiates autophagy, a cellular self-cleansing process that degrades and recycles damaged cellular components (Levine et al., 2017). Autophagy is essential for cellular maintenance and health, and its activation through prolonged fasting periods has been linked to longevity and a diminished risk of disease.

The intrigue around autophagy and intermittent fasting is truly remarkable, suggesting that extending the time we fast can enhance our body's natural renewal process, supporting cellular health and longevity. This combination of age-old wisdom and modern scientific research presents intermittent fasting as a balanced approach to health. It reconnects us with the natural cycles of our ancestors while providing a remedy to the overindulgences of contemporary diets.

Intermittent Fasting Techniques for Lifespan Extension

1. Start with the 16/8 Method

This involves fasting for 16 hours each day and eating all your meals within an 8-hour window. It's a simple, sustainable approach to intermittent fasting that can improve metabolic health and extend lifespan (Mattson et al., 2017).

2. Stay Hydrated

During fasting periods, it's crucial to stay hydrated. Water, black coffee, and tea are excellent choices that do not break a fast (Patterson & Sears, 2017).

3. Plan Nutrient-Dense Meals

When you do eat, focus on nutrient-dense foods— vegetables, fruits, lean proteins, and healthy fats. This ensures your body gets the necessary nutrients within the eating window (Varady & Hellerstein, 2007).

4. Gradually Increase Fasting Duration

If you're new to intermittent fasting, start with shorter fasting periods and gradually increase them. This helps your body adjust without causing undue stress (Anton et al., 2018).

5. Listen to Your Body

Intermittent fasting unfolds differently for everyone, and this rings especially true for women. It's essential for you to approach fasting with an awareness of your body's unique rhythms, particularly in tune with your menstrual cycle. The natural ebb and flow of hormones throughout your cycle can influence your energy, metabolism, and how your body responds to fasting.

Studies highlight that tailoring your fasting schedule to sync up with the different phases of your menstrual cycle could optimize the benefits of fasting, working hand in hand with your body's hormonal fluctuations. For example, during the follicular phase—the first stretch of your cycle starting with menstruation—rising estrogen levels might make your body more equipped to handle the stress of fasting. On the flip side, the luteal phase, marking the cycle's latter half, might present more of a challenge for fasting due to increased energy needs and appetite changes (Kumar & Kaur, 2012).

Adapting Fasting for Women

Follicular Phase: You might find it comfortable to keep or even extend your fasting period slightly, as your body may be more adaptable to fasting stress during this phase.

Luteal Phase: It could be beneficial to reduce your fasting window or introduce more nutrient-rich foods to meet your body's heightened energy and nutritional demands.

6. 3-Day Water Fasts

Imagine giving your body a complete break from food, hydrating with only water for three days. This kind of fast activates a fascinating process called autophagy, where your cells begin a self-cleaning routine, removing damaged parts and potentially lowering inflammation, rejuvenating your body from the inside out (Choi et al., 2019). Embarking on such a fast requires careful preparation, both mentally and physically, to ensure you're ready for this deep dive into cellular renewal.

7. Juice Fasts

Opting for a juice fast means nourishing yourself with fruit and vegetable juices for usually one to three days. This gentler approach still eases the workload on your digestive system, allowing your body to focus on detoxification. At the same time, you still intake vital nutrients in a liquid form. While the scientific community continues to explore the full scope of juice fasting's benefits, it's clear that using fresh, natural juices is key to avoiding excess sugars and preservatives (Henning et al., 2017).

8. Monthly 24-Hour Fasts

Adopting a 24-hour fast once a month, as suggested by health experts like Dr. Michael Mosley, offers a periodic reset for your body. This practice aims to stimulate cellular repair and enhance overall longevity with a manageable commitment, presenting a less intense but still effective way to familiarize your body with the benefits of fasting (Varady et al., 2013).

As you consider these paths to physical renewal, remember that each step you take is part of a more significant journey toward a healthier, more vibrant you. These fasting practices invite you to reconnect with your body's natural rhythms, embracing ancient wisdom through a modern lens for a vitality-filled life.

Spirituality and Longevity: The Impact of Inner Peace on Physical Health

> Inner peace is about more than just steering clear of stress; it's about cultivating a state of mental and spiritual calm, armed with the wisdom and understanding to remain steadfast and serene amidst life's challenges.

In the hustle of today's world, where achievements and material gains often take center stage, nurturing inner peace might feel like a secondary concern or even a luxury. Yet, the journey towards inner tranquility is deeply connected to our overall health and longevity.

The dialogue between spirituality and physical health has captured the curiosity of researchers for years. There's a growing pile of evidence showing that spiritual practices like meditation, prayer, and mindfulness don't just soothe the soul; they have tangible benefits for our physical health. For instance, having a purpose in life and feeling satisfied with your life can reduce your mortality risk by 17% and 12%, respectively (Dominguez, Veronese, & Barbagallo, 2024). These practices can dial down stress, lower blood pressure, boost immune function, and reduce chronic disease risk.

Take meditation and mindfulness, for instance. They do not just escape from the noise of daily life. They trigger a wave of physical changes that counteract stress's toll on the body, lowering cortisol levels and boosting your immune system. Regularly dipping into these practices can even protect our chromosomes' tips, suggesting a slower pace of aging at the cellular level.

Moreover, spirituality weaves a sense of purpose and meaning into the fabric of our lives. These threads are tightly linked to healthier and longer lives. Feeling grounded in a purpose can fend off sleep issues, heart disease, and other health troubles, adding years to your life. This sense of direction, often nurtured through spiritual exploration, acts as a shield against life's stressors, paving the way for a body that's not just surviving but thriving.

Inner Peace: An Active Journey Towards Health

Inner peace, that serene state where the mind is free from worry, anxiety, and stress, isn't just a balm for the soul; it's a cornerstone for your physical health. Studies have drawn a clear line connecting the tranquility of the mind with the vitality of the body, showing how a calm inner world can shield against illness and pave the way for a longer, healthier life. Finding inner peace is a dynamic endeavor, a path walked with mindfulness and deliberate choice. It's about embracing gratitude, compassion, and acceptance, extending these gifts to ourselves and those around us. These spiritual keystones not only lift our spirits but also bolster our emotional resilience, mitigating depression and anxiety. Here are some steps grounded in science to help you cultivate this essential serenity:

Meditation

Meditation is not just a practice but a journey towards embracing the present moment with openness and without judgment. For those new to this practice, the initial challenge of quieting the mind can be significant. This is where technology steps in as a valuable ally. Meditation apps like Insight Timer and Calm offer guided sessions that can significantly aid beginners in establishing a consistent practice. These apps provide a variety of meditations guided by experts, catering to all levels and needs, making meditation accessible and engaging. Beginning with just a few minutes a day can pave the way to a deeper connection with oneself, reducing stress and enhancing overall well-being (Goyal et al., 2014).

Mindfulness in Everyday Life

Incorporating mindfulness into daily activities can transform mundane tasks into moments of presence and awareness. Mindful walking, where attention is focused on the sensation of movement and the environment, offers an opportunity to connect with the present moment beyond the constraints of a conventional meditation environment. Similarly, engaging in chores with full awareness—paying attention to the sights, sounds, and physical sensations—can elevate these activities into mindful practices. These approaches to mindfulness ensure that the benefits of meditation extend beyond the cushion, permeating every aspect of life, and bringing a sense of calm and focus to the everyday.

Make Movement a Ritual

Physical activity is a natural antidote to stress. It sends a rush of endorphins (the happiness hormones) through your system, offering a profound and physical sense of peace (Sharma et al., 2006). Find joy in moving your body, whether it's through a brisk walk, yoga, or a swim, to nourish both mind and body.

Cultivate Connections

The strength of your social bonds is a powerful predictor of mental wellness and inner peace. Deep, meaningful connections can protect against emotional turmoil and even physical ailments (Uchino, 2006). Cherish and nurture your relationships with loved ones, and seek out communities that resonate with your spirit.

Embrace Gratitude

Gratitude opens the door to more joy, harmony, and health. Acknowledging blessings in your life can significantly boost your mood and sense of well-being (Emmons & McCullough, 2003). Consider keeping a gratitude journal to celebrate the daily significant or subtle blessings.

Choose Your News Wisely

A constant diet of negative news can fray your nerves and obscure your peace of mind. Be intentional with your media consumption, stepping away from the cycle of bad news when it becomes too much. Instead, fill your cup with stories and images that uplift and inspire you (Johnston & Davey, 1997). It's essential to approach your media consumption with awareness and purpose, choosing what enriches your mental landscape. This includes a heavy dose of TV shows and movies steeped in themes that often stoke fear. The constant flow of true crime narratives, horror stories, and the negativity that frequently colors advertising messages can deeply influence our mental state. Such a barrage of gloomy content doesn't just stir up anxiety; it can warp our view of the world into one that's more fearful and cynical. Make it a point to seek out and immerse yourself in stories, shows, and social media that breathe inspiration, joy, and a positive spirit into your day.

Breathe Deeply and Fully

The power of your breath to transform stress into peace is profound. Practices like diaphragmatic breathing, 4-7-8 breathing, or box breathing are simple yet powerful tools to bring you back to a state of calm anytime, anywhere (Ma et al., 2017). An intriguing aspect of breathwork that you'll find captivating is its ability to positively impact stem cell regeneration, primarily through techniques like breath retention after exhaling, known as Nisshesha Rechaka Pranayama (Malshe, 2011). This specific method of breath control introduces brief periods of intermittent hypoxia (momentarily reduced oxygen levels), sparking adaptive bodily responses that boost stem cell migration and regeneration. A growing number of people have experienced significant relief from physical discomforts and pains after engaging in breathwork sessions, highlighting a therapeutic connection between targeted breathing exercises and pain alleviation. This effect might stem from the decrease in stress-related hormones and the enhancement of the body's relaxation responses, which could, in turn, ease pain symptoms. Research on "Nisshesha Rechaka Pranayama" demonstrates benefits derived from brief intermittent hypoxia. It also reveals how this practice can stimulate the production of essential factors like erythropoietin and vascular endothelial growth factor, which are crucial for health and healing. These findings showcase breathwork's profound influence on your health and aging (Malshe, 2011).

Reconnect with Nature

Mother Nature is a healer, offering her calm and resilience freely. Research shows that time spent in green spaces can lower your stress levels, boost your mood, and contribute to physical well-being (Hartig et al., 2014). Let nature's peace flow through you, whether it's a leisurely park walk, tending to a garden, or simply basking in the sun.

Embrace Simplicity for a Serene Mind

Clear out the clutter from your living and workspace to invite calmness into your life. An orderly environment paves the way for a tranquil mind. Learn to gracefully decline tasks and commitments that don't resonate with your core values or that stretch your resources too thin. Honoring what's genuinely important to you brings clarity and peace.

Find Joy in Creativity

Channeling your emotions into creative outlets like painting, writing, or music is a beautiful way to find inner calm. These activities offer a safe space to express yourself and melt away stress. Carve out moments in your week dedicated to hobbies or activities that ignite your creative spark and bring you happiness.

Cultivate Forgiveness

Letting go of old grudges and forgiving others—and yourself—lifts a heavy emotional burden. Reflect on past hurts to release them, freeing your heart and mind for peace.

Establish Healthy Boundaries

Setting clear personal boundaries is essential for safeguarding your peace. It's about lovingly communicating your limits regarding your time, energy, and emotional well-being. Express your boundaries with kindness and firmness, ensuring they are honored by those around you.

Seek Support When Needed

If inner peace feels elusive, especially when grappling with deeper emotional or mental health issues, reaching out for professional help is a sign of strength. A therapist or counselor can offer valuable tools and perspectives for overcoming these hurdles. Moreover, if you find yourself at a crossroads or in search of deep life transformations, considering transformational coaching could be life-changing. Whether it's a life coach, spiritual mentor, or business coach you seek, they provide the guidance, accountability, and encouragement needed to unlock your full potential and bring about substantial changes in your life.

Nurture Positive Inner Dialogue

Cultivating a positive self-dialogue goes beyond simply being optimistic; it's a crucial step toward embracing self-love and compassion. The conversations you have with yourself play a pivotal role in shaping your emotional and mental landscape. Embedding self-love and compassion into these inner discussions is vital for fostering meaningful transformation in your life. This process starts with recognizing your inherent value, embracing your imperfections, and celebrating your victories, regardless of size.

To nurture a kinder, more compassionate inner voice, identify the critical voices within and consciously counteract negative thoughts with kindness and empathy. For example, if you find yourself dwelling on a mistake, gently remind yourself that every misstep is a chance for growth and learning. Lean into affirmations highlighting your worth and resilience, like "I am deserving of love and joy" or "I am doing my best, and that's completely okay."

Adopting self-compassion means treating yourself with the same kindness and understanding you'd offer a close friend. It involves allowing yourself to be human—flawed and fabulous—and prioritizing your well-being. This gentle approach can revolutionize your relationship with yourself and influence how you face life's hurdles. Practice steering these internal dialogues towards positivity, recognizing your strengths and the strides you've made towards peace.

Embrace the Calm of Aromatherapy

The soothing power of scents like lavender, chamomile, or sandalwood can help ease the mind. Incorporate aromatherapy into your daily routine through diffusers, candles, or topical oils, creating a sanctuary of calm.

Connect with Animals

Spending time with pets or animals can be incredibly soothing, offering a unique source of joy and companionship. Whether it's cuddling with your pet or enjoying the simple pleasure of watching wildlife, these connections can be deeply comforting.

The quest for inner peace transcends spiritual fulfillment; it's a strategic path towards better health and a longer, more joyous life. Through the calm brought on by spiritual practices, we unlock a trove of health benefits, from stress relief and immune support to a profound sense of life's purpose. Embracing spirituality is not just a journey of the heart; it's a journey of the body, mind, and spirit, guiding us towards a life lived fully and deeply.

What's Next?

This chapter may have taken you on an enlightening journey to understand the essence of a life lived fully and long. I went gracefully through the science of aging, separating fact from fiction and discovering the genuine elements that fuel our longevity. From the inspiring stories of the world's Blue Zones to the cutting-edge approaches of biohacking, you learned that enhancing your well-being is a tangible goal. Our exploration into spirituality revealed the powerful connection between a peaceful inner world and our physical health, offering practical ways to weave serenity into our everyday existence.

Now, as you step into Chapter 2, I'm ready to deepen your understanding with concrete, day-to-day practices that feed both body and soul. This chapter is your companion in detailing the vital ingredients of a life well-lived, focusing on nourishing diets, personalized exercise plans, the restorative magic of sleep, and mastering the art of stress management. Each segment is carefully designed to arm you with the insights and means to cultivate a harmonious, health-oriented lifestyle. As you navigate through these essential building blocks, remember, the path to enduring vitality isn't paved with sudden, radical shifts. Instead, it's about welcoming gentle, lasting changes that bloom into a more prosperous, vibrant existence.

CHAPTER 2

Building Blocks For Healthy Aging

"Only 20 percent of our longevity is genetically determined. The rest is what we do, how we live our lives and increasingly the molecules that we take. It's not the loss of our DNA that causes aging, it's the problems in reading the information, the epigenetic noise."

- David Andrew Sinclair

This perspective by Sinclair reaffirms what I've realized over the years. The external effects of aging are less dictated by the linear progression of time and more influenced by the cumulative impact of daily health decisions. It's a revelation of my control over my vitality and longevity, where genetics only sketch the outline of my life's potential.

In this chapter, I explore how to actively engage in lengthening your health span with deliberate practices and habits. From appreciating the restorative power of sleep and learning stress management techniques to customizing your exercise routine to adapt to your body's changes over the years, each section aims to steer you towards a life brimming with energy and vibrance.

The goal transcends merely increasing your lifespan; it's about enriching the quality of every year. By taking a holistic approach to nutrition and well-being, you can minimize the negative influences on your genes (epigenetic noise), allowing your body's natural potential to shine through for a longer lifespan, as Sinclair suggests. I invite you to join me on this exploration as we discover how to fine-tune our bodies and minds to the melody of enduring youth. The upcoming pages will reveal the keys to a nourished existence, empowering you to approach aging with elegance, resilience, and zeal.

Nourishing Your Body Well: A Detailed Guide to Anti-Aging Nutrition

Centuries back, Hippocrates, the pioneer of modern medicine, wisely stated, "Let food be thy medicine." It highlights your diet's critical role in sustaining health and extending longevity. In our modern pursuit of youthfulness, grasping the complex dance between the foods you consume and your body's aging process is more important than ever.

The Double-Edged Sword of Free Radicals

On a molecular level, your body is a dynamic arena where antioxidants and free radicals clash. In small numbers, free radicals, unstable molecules that serve vital roles like combating infections, become harmful when their levels rise unchecked. This surplus triggers oxidative stress, leading to cellular harm. Such imbalances speed up aging and are the culprits behind chronic conditions, including heart diseases and cancer (Pham-Huy et al., 2008).

Antioxidants stand as your body's line of defense against the detrimental effects of free radicals. They safeguard your cells by donating one of their electrons to stabilize free radicals, thereby preventing cellular damage. Keeping this balance between antioxidants and free radicals is essential for your health and gracefully slows down the aging clock (Pham-Huy et al., 2008).

The Role of Diet in Balancing Free Radicals

Embracing a diet that's rich in antioxidants is my strategy to fight oxidative stress. Consuming foods like berries, nuts, dark leafy greens, and fish, which are packed with antioxidants such as vitamins C and E, selenium, and flavonoids, empower you to counteract the harmful influence of free radicals (Pandey & Rizvi, 2009).

Although a balanced diet should be your primary source of antioxidants, supplements can complement your nutritional arsenal, ensuring you receive ample antioxidants. Yet, it's vital you don't lean solely on supplements for your antioxidant needs. Whole foods bring a complex array of nutrients, fiber, and antioxidants that synergistically enhance health, a harmony isolated supplements can't mimic (Bjelakovic et al., 2012).

Steering your diet towards antioxidant-rich foods can markedly diminish the wear and tear caused by free radicals, thereby decelerating aging and cutting down the risk of chronic diseases. I'm inspired by Hippocrates's wisdom to let food be my medicine, with supplements serving as an auxiliary, not the bedrock of my anti-aging regimen.

Actionable Steps

To craft a diet that effectively wards off aging, I've learned that adopting specific, actionable strategies can vastly enhance my overall health and longevity:

Incorporate More Antioxidant-Rich Foods

Antioxidants are your allies in neutralizing free radicals, slashing oxidative stress, and decelerating the aging process. Fill your plate with at least five servings of fruits and vegetables daily. Your go-to antioxidant powerhouses should include:

- Berries like blueberries, strawberries, and raspberries
- Leafy greens, such as spinach, kale, and Swiss chard
- Nuts including walnuts and almonds
- Seeds like flaxseeds and chia seeds
- Orange vegetables, such as carrots and sweet potatoes

Think About Anti-Aging Supplements

While your primary nutrition source should always be whole foods, you can incorporate certain supplements as well. It's wise to chat with healthcare professionals to pinpoint which supplements could be beneficial for you, especially those teeming with antioxidants like Vitamin C, Vitamin E, Selenium, and Omega-3 fatty acids. Remember, supplements are there to complement your diet, not substitute it, filling in any nutritional voids (Bjelakovic et al., 2012).

Stay Hydrated with Filtered Water

Keeping hydrated is crucial in eliminating toxins from your body, which in turn contributes to healthier skin and overall well-being. Aim for at least eight glasses of water a day, and consider investing in a quality water filter. Purifying your water can strip away harmful chemicals and contaminants, ensuring you're quenching your thirst with the cleanest water possible, a vital step for peak health (Popkin, D'Anci, & Rosenberg, 2010).

Reduce Your Intake of Processed Foods

Processed foods come packed with sugars, unhealthy fats, and unwanted additives that can fast-forward aging. Such foods fuel inflammation and oxidative stress, paving the way for chronic diseases and an accelerated aging timeline. To further enhance your health and longevity, consider the next level of dietary mindfulness: opting for organic and locally grown foods. By prioritizing fresh, whole foods, you minimize exposure to genetically modified organisms (GMOs) and ensure your meals retain the maximum nutrient content that can be lost during long-term cold storage. Make it a goal to limit processed foods, leaning instead toward whole, nutrient-rich foods that support both optimal health and longevity (Ludwig, 2011).

Incorporating these practices into your daily life can enhance your vitality and pave the way for a long, flourishing existence.

Exercise for Every Age: Tailored Fitness Routines for Enhanced Lifespan

Throughout human history, movement has been a cornerstone of our evolution. Your ancestors, constantly on the go as hunters and gatherers, didn't know the sedentary lifestyle you might find familiar today. This constant activity shaped our bodies to need and thrive on movement—starkly contrasting today's norm of sitting for long hours with little physical effort. It highlights a crucial fact: your body is designed to move. It benefits immensely from regular activity, no matter your age.

Age Is Merely a Number; Staying Active Is Essential for Health

Indeed, "age is just a number" couldn't be more accurate regarding staying active. Your body, irrespective of its age, possesses a remarkable ability to adapt and grow stronger with exercise. Regular physical activity is vital to preserving and improving your health, enhancing cardiovascular functions, strengthening muscles and bones, and even boosting mental health by alleviating depression and anxiety.

Incorporating exercise into your routine shouldn't feel like a chore. It's about finding joy and balance in activities that fit your current physical condition and preferences. For the younger crowd, intense exercises like running, cycling, or team sports may appeal. As you grow older, you lean towards gentler forms of exercise such as walking, swimming, yoga, or tai chi, which keep you fit while minimizing injury risks. Physical activities like dancing, gardening, or walking your dog echo the principles found in the Blue Zones, where exercise is naturally interwoven into everyday life instead of being a structured task. In places like Okinawa, Japan, and Sardinia, Italy, people naturally maintain their activity levels through their daily habits, such as the frequent movement from sitting on the floor to standing or treading their hilly towns.

Napoleon Hill once said, "The body achieves what the mind believes." Let this thought light your way, regardless age, towards a healthier, more active lifestyle. The first step is to believe in your body's capacity to adapt and improve through exercise. By marrying this belief with our innate need for movement, you unlock endless potential for health, vitality, and a long life. Physical activity should be a fundamental part of your health strategy, customized to your age and physical ability, to extend your lifespan and quality of life. It's never too late to begin, and the rewards of movement go well beyond physical benefits, enriching every aspect of your life.

> Embrace the truth that to move is to live, guiding you towards wellness and vibrancy at every stage of life.

Exercise Routines

Adopting an exercise routine that matches your age and physical condition isn't just beneficial—it's essential for amplifying your health benefits while minimizing risks. Your exercise plan should be personalized given the variety of individual health, abilities, and interests. Here are some tailored recommendations for different stages of your life:

Children & Teenagers

Getting active in these crucial years builds a foundation for lifelong health and wellness. Sports and fun, engaging activities can boost your physical strength, coordination, and heart health, all while fostering social skills and teamwork. Activities like soccer, basketball, swimming, and martial arts are fantastic for developing your agility, strength, and endurance. For those who may not resonate with traditional sports, discovering joy in activities like climbing, biking, dog walking, skating, hiking, or playful outings to the pool is vital. Emphasizing fun in movement helps prevent negative associations, fostering a healthy, active lifestyle far beyond these formative years.

Adults

Adult life often leans towards a sedentary lifestyle, highlighting the importance of integrating a balanced exercise routine. A mix of cardiovascular workouts and strength training is vital for keeping your heart healthy, muscles strong, and bones dense. If you fret about doing this alone, find a partner and make it fun. Doing this with a family member or friend will not only keep you motivated but will also help develop strong bonds and relationships. Including flexibility and core-strengthening exercises, such as Yoga and Pilates, can enhance your posture, ease stress, and prevent injuries. Stretching and maintaining hip mobility are crucial for longevity, improving flexibility, and reducing injury risks. Recent insights suggest that using rollers for myofascial release can be even more effective than traditional stretching by targeting muscle fascia, thereby improving flexibility and decreasing injury rates.

For You, the Seniors

Maintaining mobility, flexibility, and balance is crucial in healthy aging. Engaging in low-impact exercises that focus on these areas can significantly improve your life's quality. Tai chi and Chi Gong are incredibly beneficial, blending gentle physical movement with mindfulness to lower fall risks, boost mental health, and improve overall well-being. Additionally, practices like chair yoga and aqua aerobics, which are gentle on the joints, are also highly beneficial for seniors, promoting strength, balance, and cardiovascular health (Page, 2012; Cheatham, Kolber, & Cain, 2015). These practices have been shown to enhance balance and stability, ease arthritis symptoms, and support heart health.

Exercise is a powerful, versatile tool for health at any age. However, it's not a one-size-fits-all solution. By tailoring physical activity to meet your specific needs and stage of life, you can maximize the benefits of your efforts.

The Principle of Consistency

In the world of fitness and longevity, the mantra "consistency over intensity" serves as a guiding light. This philosophy underscores that the real rewards of exercise come when it's woven consistently into the fabric of your life rather than in occasional, intense efforts. Following the World Health Organization's (WHO) advice, regular moderate-intensity physical activities are the key to warding off chronic diseases and boosting your health at every stage of life.

Exercise Tips for Your Lifelong Wellness

As you tread on your journey towards lifelong wellness, exercise stands out as a cornerstone, essential for nurturing your physical and mental health. Your approach should be tailored, mindful, and progressive. Here's what you can do;

Begin Gradually

If exercise hasn't been a staple in your routine, start gently. Research in the Journal of American Medicine shows that even regular activities of low intensity can markedly reduce your risk of heart disease (Lee & Skerrett, 2001). Choose exercises that match your current fitness level and slowly elevate the duration and intensity.

Tune Into Your Body

Paying attention to how your body feels is crucial. If you experience pain or discomfort, it might signal that you're pushing too hard or need a different exercise approach. This awareness can help you avoid injuries, making exercise a sustainable and enjoyable part of your life.

Prioritize Hydration

Staying hydrated is vital for your best performance and recovery. According to the American College of Sports Medicine, you should drink fluids before, during, and after exercise to maintain hydration and support your overall health (Casa et al., 2000).

Don't Skip Warm-Ups and Cool-Downs

Initiating your workout with a warm-up boosts your heart rate and blood flow to muscles. At the same time, a cool-down phase helps your body gradually return to its pre-exercise state, minimizing muscle stiffness and soreness. Both steps are non-negotiable for a safe and effective workout routine (American College of Sports Medicine, 2011).

Inspiring Stories of Transformation

There are countless stories of people who have turned their health around through consistent exercise. For example, research shows that you can effectively manage type 2 diabetes by making physical activity a regular part of their lives (Colberg et al., 2010). These success stories highlight the transformative potential of exercise—not only as a preventive strategy but as a powerful tool for regaining health.

Your path to a healthier, more vibrant life is paved with regular, moderate-intensity exercise. This journey is open to everyone, regardless of age or current fitness level, enriched by listening to your body, ensuring hydration, and recognizing the critical roles of warming up and cooling down.

Rejuvenating Sleep Patterns: Decoding the Role of Rest in Anti-Aging

The interplay between sleep and aging is a fascinating area of study that reveals just how crucial rest is to our biological functions. Sleep isn't just downtime; it's critical to regulating your health and longevity. It works at the cellular level to slow aging and boost your well-being.

The Science Behind Your Sleep & Aging

Quality sleep is essential for several physiological processes that play a big part in aging gracefully. While asleep, your body is busy repairing and rejuvenating, clearing out neurotoxic waste from your brain, which helps ward off neurodegenerative diseases. Moreover, sleep helps regulate hormones that manage your appetite, stress, and growth, and repair cellular damage from free radicals (Walker, 2017). These actions are vital for keeping your metabolism in check and staving off age-related declines.

Quality Sleep as Your Anti-Aging Ally

Quality sleep is more than just the key to waking up feeling refreshed; it's a cornerstone of your body's anti-aging defense. It helps preserve the length of your telomeres, and guards against DNA damage. It boosts your immune function, contributing to slowing down aging at the cellular level (Cappuccio et al., 2010).

It's a common myth that you need less sleep as you age. While it's true that sleep patterns can change with age, the need for restorative sleep does not diminish. Often, difficulties in getting quality rest as you age are linked more to health issues than to a decrease in sleep necessity. Tackling these sleep challenges is crucial for maintaining health and functionality (Hood & Amir, 2017).

Revitalizing Your Sleep Preparation Tips

As you might remember from Chapter 1, gearing up for quality sleep involves keeping a regular sleep schedule, creating a peaceful environment devoid of electronic interruptions, and indulging in calming pre-sleep routines. These strategies are valuable for people of any age and foster restorative sleep initiation and quality.

Thanks to technological advances, tracking your sleep patterns at home has never been easier. Gadgets like Fitbit and other sleep trackers provide insights into how long and well you sleep, including any disturbances. Moreover, subjective measures, like how rejuvenated you feel upon waking and during the day, offer important clues about the state of your sleep health. Utilizing these tools can pinpoint areas needing improvement and gauge the success of adjustments to your sleep routine.

Stress Management Techniques For Better Aging: Achieving Emotional Balance and Mental Clarity

Stress, often called the 'silent assassin,' deeply impacts your well-being and how gracefully you age. Although stress is a natural part of life, when it becomes chronic, it can lead to serious health issues, including heart problems, a weakened immune system, and accelerated aging at a cellular level. Learning to manage your stress is vital to maintaining emotional balance and mental clarity as you grow older.

Understanding the Fight or Flight Response

Your body's fight or flight response is a primal reaction to perceived threats, priming you either to stand your ground or escape. In today's world, this response can be triggered by stressors that aren't directly life-threatening, such as job pressures or personal conflicts, leading to chronic stress. This constant state of alert can wreak havoc on your body, disrupting almost every system (McEwen, 2007).

Managing stress isn't just about finding calm in the moment; it's about building a life where peace is your baseline.

Deepak Chopra wisely points out, "Remember that stress is not what happens to you, but your response to what happens to you." This insight highlights the importance of your reaction to stress and the effectiveness of proactive stress management.

Self-Awareness and Identifying Your Stress Triggers

The first step to emotional balance is self-awareness—knowing what triggers your stress and understanding how you react to various stressors. Building a solid self-care routine is crucial for managing stress. This means recognizing stress symptoms early and allowing yourself to engage in self-care practices through meditation, physical activity, pursuing hobbies, or practicing relaxation techniques (Sutton, 2016).

Acknowledging the need to prioritize your well-being is essential. Only when you're in a state of equilibrium can you truly offer the best of yourself to others? Making your health and well-being a priority benefits your aging process and enhances your interactions and contributions to those around you.

Stress Management

In your quest for a life filled with grace and vitality, mastering stress management is not just helpful—it's vital. Chronic stress can deeply affect your physical health, emotional balance, and mental clarity. To navigate this, here are essential strategies to manage stress effectively:

1. Pinpoint the Specific Sources of Your Stress

The initial step towards conquering stress is to identify and understand the exact stressors in your life. This demands introspection and honesty about what really triggers your stress, be it work deadlines, financial worries, or personal relationships. Maintaining a stress journal can prove to be incredibly helpful. You'll notice patterns and common stressors by documenting moments of stress and identifying triggers. Recognizing these triggers is crucial in stress management, as it allows you to create focused strategies to tackle or avoid these stress inducers (Smyth et al., 2018).

2. Make Regular Physical Activity Part of Your Day

Physical activity is an exceptional stress buster. It's not solely about aerobic workouts; any form of physical activity can boost your health and sense of well-being, thus mitigating stress. Activities like walking, jogging, swimming, or dancing can release endorphins, your body's happiness hormones. Regular physical activity demonstrably reduces overall stress levels, enhances and stabilizes mood, improves sleep quality, and bolsters self-esteem. Remarkably, just five minutes of aerobic activity can have anti-anxiety effects (Anderson & Shivakumar, 2013).

3. Embrace Mindfulness Techniques like Meditation or Yoga

Mindfulness and meditation are proven to significantly lower stress and alleviate symptoms of various conditions, including anxiety, depression, and chronic pain. These practices encourage you to focus on the present, helping you gain a fresh perspective on stressful situations. Yoga merges physical movement with breathing exercises and meditation, offering a comprehensive method for stress relief. Regularly practicing mindfulness and yoga diminishes stress and elevates your overall sense of well-being (Goyal et al., 2014).

4. Nourish Your Body with a Balanced Diet and Prioritize Your Sleep

Eating a balanced diet fills you with essential nutrients, bolstering both your physical health and emotional resilience against stress. Foods rich in omega-3 fatty acids, like salmon and walnuts, have been noted to dial down stress levels and elevate your mood (Gómez-Pinilla, 2008). At the same time, complex carbohydrates from whole grains can stabilize your blood sugar levels, indirectly managing your stress responses. It's crucial to avoid high-sugar and high-fat foods, which can amplify stress and harm your health.

Getting enough sleep is just as crucial; it's the golden time when your body embarks on self-repair, cements memories, and balances your emotions. A lack of sleep can make you more susceptible to stress and muddle your emotional regulation, making it harder to handle stress. You should aim for 7-9 hours of quality sleep each night, sticking to a regular sleep schedule and crafting a peaceful, electronics-free sleeping environment to enhance your sleep quality (Walker, 2017).

5. Regularly Connect with Friends, Family, or Support Groups

Social connections are a cornerstone in stress management and enhancing your lifespan. Keeping in touch with friends, family, or support groups offers a sense of belonging and acts as a potent stress buster. Discussing your experiences with those who get you and offer support can alleviate stress, open new viewpoints, and lend emotional backing during tough times. Moreover, engaging with others can lift your spirits and lessen feelings of loneliness, which is crucial for your mental well-being. Research shows that people with robust social networks often enjoy longer, healthier lives, highlighting the need to nurture these bonds (Holt-Lunstad, Smith, & Layton, 2010).

6. Seek Professional Help If Stress Becomes Overbearing

Sometimes, despite your best efforts, stress might become too much, heavily influencing your day-to-day life and health. When you find yourself in such situations, seeking professional guidance is essential. Therapists, psychologists, and counselors can offer tailored strategies for managing stress effectively. They can also delve into any deeper issues fueling your stress, guiding you towards lasting emotional and mental wellness (Ratini, 2023). Remember, seeking help is a sign of strength and a proactive measure in safeguarding your health and enhancing your life quality.

What's Next?

I sincerely hope Chapter 2 has set the stage for a vibrant and enduring life. You discovered the pivotal roles of personalized exercise, restorative sleep patterns, and effective stress management, each acting as a cornerstone to bolster your quest for optimal aging. From understanding the science of underpinning your daily habits to pinpointing actionable steps for enhancement, this chapter has armed you with a thorough guide to elevate your quality of life and extend your years of active, healthful living.

As you turn the page, get ready to get into the essence of thriving well. This next chapter is poised to unfold a wealth of knowledge and practices aimed at elevating your wellness journey. Here, you'll tap into the transformative essence of mindfulness practices, discovering how being fully present can saturate your life with vibrancy and markedly contribute to your longevity. The profound effects of mindfulness and presence on your well-being will be laid bare, offering you a clear vision of their impact.

You're also set to cleanse and refresh with detoxification routines, learning the ropes of purifying your system for peak health. This section will walk you through practical strategies to rid your body of toxins, boosting your natural healing capabilities and rejuvenating your entire being.

But the exploration doesn't end there. Chapter 3 will guide you through holistic healing methods, including acupuncture, yoga, and meditation. These practices present a unified approach to wellness, nurturing your mind, body, and spirit together. You'll learn to seamlessly weave these time-honored techniques into your contemporary life, finding balance and holistic well-being. As we journey together through these pages, stay open to the profound changes these practices can bring, ready to adopt healthy habits that pave the way to a timeless, vibrant existence.

CHAPTER 3

Cultivating Healthy Habits For Timeless Living

"He who has health, has hope; and he who has hope, has everything."

– Arabian Proverb

This Arabian proverb captures the essence of living a life brimming with vibrant health and well-being. As you flip through the following pages, you'll dive into practices honed over thousands of years, designed to nurture your body, mind, and spirit. Plus, you'll discover the transformative power of mindfulness practices, learning how being fully present can significantly enrich the quality of your life and aid in your journey toward longevity.

In today's era, where toxins constantly surround us, mastering the art of cleansing and rejuvenation is crucial in sustaining vitality and warding off illness. I'll unpack detoxification routines for you, helping you comprehend the critical role of purifying your system for peak health. Moreover, you'll delve into holistic healing methods like acupuncture, yoga, and meditation to achieve overall bodily harmony. These time-tested practices promise deep benefits, from reducing stress and alleviating pain to boosting mental clarity and emotional stability.

> Cultivating healthy habits is not going to help anyone, but you. You will not just add years to your life but also life to your years.

If this idea sounds interesting, I urge you to read through it with an open heart and mind and let this chapter be your guide to integrating mindfulness, detoxification, and holistic healing into a lifestyle of timeless living.

Mindfulness Practices: Staying Present for a Vibrant Life

Mindfulness, the art of staying fully present and immersed in the now without casting judgment, stands as a formidable ally in bolstering your well-being. Jim Rohn gracefully stated,

"Take care of your body. It's the only place you have to live."

Underlining the critical importance of mindfulness in your everyday life. This wisdom beckons you to be acutely aware of both your physical and mental health, embracing the present with open arms. Mindfulness serves as a beacon for both your mind and body, easing stress, sharpening your focus, and fostering emotional stability. It bridges the gap between your physical being and your mental processes, paving the way for enhanced overall health (Kabat-Zinn, 2003). Embracing mindfulness invites a symphony of benefits into your life, enriching your existence with clarity, peace, and resilience.

Mindfulness, Presence, and Their Impact on Longevity

Your journey towards a long and vibrant life is a balance between diet, environment, and mental health. Mindfulness and presence are key to shaping your choices and behaviors in ways that nourish your existence. Research hints at the promising impacts of mindfulness meditation on key indicators of inflammation, cell-mediated immunity, and biological aging. However, while meditation offers a lot of general benefits, these specific outcomes are preliminary and call for additional studies to confirm their validity. (David & George 2016)

The Connection Between Diet, Environment, and Mental Health

Mindful eating transforms your approach to food, emphasizing quality and origin, encouraging you to make nutritious and kind choices to the planet. This act of conscious consumption bolsters your physical health. It lessens your ecological footprint, illustrating how diet, mental health, and environmental care are intertwined (Willett et al., 2019). Your surrounding environment, both physical and social, impacts your mental well-being. From keeping your living areas clean to nurturing quality relationships, mindfulness invites you to cultivate spaces that radiate peace and wellness. A supportive and uplifting environment can lower stress and boost joy, paving the way for a fulfilling life (Kondo & Flaxman, 2018).

The Perks of Being Mindfully Present

Beyond extending your years, living with a full mental and mindful presence brings an abundance of benefits.

- It's linked to less anxiety and depression, sharper cognitive functions, and better emotional control (Goyal et al., 2014). This heightened awareness fosters empathy and compassion, deepening your connections and enriching your interactions with others (Condon et al., 2013).
- Mindfulness practices, such as meditation and mindful breathing, also positively influence your physical health, helping lower blood pressure, boost immune response, and ease chronic pain (Black & Slavich, 2016).

Cultivating mindfulness and presence doesn't just enhance your personal well-being; it's a comprehensive approach that envelops diet, environment, and mental health—all crucial for a long, joyous life.

Achievable Steps for Incorporating Mindfulness

Integrating mindfulness into your everyday life improves your current quality of life and also lays the groundwork for a future prosperous in health, happiness, and longevity. Below, I've outlined a few tips and tricks so you can be on your way to a mindful start each day, week after week.

1. Start with Short, Focused Breathing Sessions

If you're pressed for time, I recommend beginning with just two minutes of focused breathing each morning. Initiating the day with two minutes of concentrated breathing can significantly impact stress reduction and mental clarity (Burzler et al., 2019). This manageable start can help soothe the stress of the day ahead and cultivate a moment of serenity.

How To Practice: Try setting a timer each morning, find a quiet spot, close your eyes, and pay attention solely to your breathing, feeling each breath as it flows in and out of your body. This simple practice anchors your mind and gently introduces you to mindfulness in an approachable manner.

As you breathe in deeply, imagine drawing in calmness and peace. As you exhale, imagine stress and tensions dissolving into the air. This combination of breathwork and visualization can significantly amplify the calming effects (Jerath et al., 2015).

2. Incorporate Mindful Eating into One Meal a Day

I encourage you to pick one meal or snack daily to eat mindfully, away from the distractions of television or smartphones. Mindful eating has been shown to enhance the eating experience and foster a healthier relationship with food (Warren et al., 2017). This practice also underscores the value of nourishment beyond mere consumption.

How To Practice: Make your meals an opportunity for mindfulness by engaging all your senses. Before eating, look at your food and appreciate its colors and composition. Smell its aromas, and as you take a bite, notice the texture and flavors on your tongue. Chew slowly, savoring each bite and paying attention to the experience of eating. This practice can transform eating from a routine activity to a rich, sensory experience, promoting better digestion and meal satisfaction (Hanley et al., 2015).

3. Introduce a Gratitude Journal

I suggest ending your day by jotting down three things you're thankful for, no matter how small. Why? Writing down three things you are grateful for each day can shift the focus from daily stresses to positivity, promoting mental well-being (Emmons & Mishra, 2011), reinforcing the mindfulness tenet of living in the present, and appreciating every moment's worth.

How To Practice: Your gratitude journal should be your own thing. You can use notebook or download an app on your phone or tablet. Find a cozy spot where you can relax and write without any distractions. Pick a daily time that works for you, whether it's a morning mood-booster or a calming reflection before bed (Mosunic, 2024). The key is to make it a habit!

4. Guided Mindfulness Meditation

For those new to meditation, beginning with guided sessions from apps or online can offer a supportive and structured approach, making meditation feel more approachable (Goyal et al., 2014). I encourage you to try various styles to discover what truly speaks to you, reminding you that there's no "right" way to meditate.

How To Practice: Select an ordinary object from your surroundings and focus on it for a few minutes. This could be a leaf, a cup of coffee, or even your own hands. Observe it as if you are seeing it for the first time, noticing every detail, texture, and color. This exercise trains your mind to be curious and engaged with the present, fostering a deeper appreciation for simple moments every day.

5. Mindful Movement

Try blending mindful walks into your daily routine. Even a brief 10-minute stroll, where you consciously observe your surroundings and tune into your body's movements, can be a potent mindfulness exercise. Incorporating mindful walks into the daily routine can merge physical activity with mindfulness, enhancing both mental and physical health (Calogiuri & Chroni, 2014).

How To Practice: You can transform a simple walk into a mindful exploration. Choose a natural setting, if possible, and fully immerse yourself in the experience as you walk. Notice the feel of the ground under your feet, the sounds of birds or rustling leaves, and the play of sunlight through the trees. This practice will not only ground you in the present moment but also deepen your connection to nature, enhancing feelings of well-being (Mackenzie & Brymer, 2018).

Detoxification Routines: Purifying your System for Optimal Health

In today's era, where the drive for more and better products has led to the exploitation of Earth's resources, we've ironically been harming ourselves and life as we know it on this planet. I discussed earlier how free radicals can wreak havoc on our organs and accelerate aging. Detoxification is a critical countermeasure designed to purge these toxins and enhance your body's innate cleansing capabilities. This concept is deeply embedded in both time-honored health practices and modern holistic approaches. Fortunately for us, our bodies are equipped with an impressive squad of detox warriors—the liver, kidneys, digestive system, skin, and lungs—all naturally designed to keep us detoxified. Yet, the lifestyle choices we make and the environments we inhabit often introduce more toxins than our bodies are equipped to handle. To support our well-being, incorporating detoxification routines can be highly beneficial (Klein & Kiat, 2014).

A study by Smith et al. (2016) underscores the profound impact of a balanced diet rich in antioxidants on enhancing immune function, thereby contributing to longevity and reducing the risk of chronic diseases. Furthermore, research by Johnson and Lee (2016) highlights the benefits of regular physical activity in improving mental well-being and cognitive function. This reinforces the idea that physical and mental health are interconnected, both crucial for a fulfilling life.

A practical detox routine can be simple and does not require extreme measures. Here's a holistic approach with actionable steps that can be easily integrated into daily life.

Start Your Day with Water and Lemon: Start each morning by drinking a glass of warm water with freshly squeezed lemon. This simple habit can kick-start digestion and liver function, promoting the body's natural detoxification processes.

Incorporate Anti-Inflammatory Foods: Focus on a diet rich in anti-inflammatory foods, such as leafy greens, berries, nuts, and seeds. These foods are packed with antioxidants and nutrients that support detoxification and overall health (Liu, 2013).

Limit Processed Foods and Sugars: Reducing the intake of processed foods, sugars, and unhealthy fats can lower the burden on your detoxification systems. Opt for whole, natural foods whenever possible to support your body's health.

Stay Hydrated: Adequate hydration is crucial for detoxification. Aim to drink at least eight glasses of water daily to help flush toxins from your body through urine and sweat.

Engage in Regular Physical Activity: Exercise stimulates blood circulation and lymphatic flow, enhancing the body's natural detoxification capabilities. Incorporate activities you enjoy, such as walking, yoga, or cycling, into your routine.

Practice Mindfulness and Stress Reduction: Chronic stress can impede the body's ability to detoxify effectively. Mindfulness practices, such as meditation and deep-breathing exercises, can reduce stress and support detoxification (Goyal et al., 2014).

Sleep Well: Quality sleep is essential for the body's healing and detoxification processes. Ensure you get 7-9 hours of sleep per night to support your body's natural rhythms and detoxification (Watson et al., 2018).

Integrating these detoxification routines and holistic practices into your lifestyle can improve energy levels, clearer skin, better digestion, and a stronger immune system, laying the foundation for a life of ageless vitality.

Next, I'll dive into holistic healing methods, such as acupuncture, yoga, and meditation. These practices are known to promote detoxification and ageless vitality. These practices help balance the body and mind, reduce stress, and enhance the body's natural healing capabilities. Yoga, for instance, promotes detoxification through specific poses that stimulate organs, improve digestion, and facilitate toxin elimination through sweat (Ross & Thomas, 2010).

Holistic Healing Methods: Nurturing Ageless Vitality

Holistic healing methods treat you as a complete being, weaving together your mind, body, and spirit to foster peak health and well-being. This approach goes beyond tackling specific symptoms or illnesses like conventional medicine. Instead, it seeks to uncover and remedy the underlying causes of imbalance, igniting healing and vitality from within.

Acupuncture & Its Principles

Acupuncture, a cornerstone of traditional Chinese medicine,

employs the use of slender needles, which are inserted into precise acupuncture points on your body. This technique aims to regulate the flow of your energy or life force, referred to as Qi or Chi, based on the philosophy that good health springs from a perfect harmony between Yin and Yang—opposing forces in the universe. Acupuncture strives to rebalance these forces, encouraging your body's innate ability to heal itself. For instance, acupuncture has effectively relieved pain, reduced stress and anxiety, improved sleep quality, and boosted overall well-being (Vickers et al., 2018). These benefits, in turn, can lead to a more vibrant and energetic life, promoting longevity and healthy aging.

Qi and Meridians: Imagine Qi as the vital energy that animates your body, crucial for your health and zest for life. Meridians serve as the channels that carry this life force throughout your body. Traditional Chinese Medicine (TCM) teaches that any disruptions or imbalances in the flow of Qi can lead to health issues. Acupuncture seeks to resolve these imbalances by targeting specific acupuncture points, thus rejuvenating the flow of Qi and bolstering your body's innate ability to heal itself.

Acupuncture Points: Your body is home to hundreds of acupuncture points, each offering unique healing properties. These points lie on or just beneath your skin's surface, positioned along the meridians. When a skilled acupuncturist places fine, sterile needles into these points, it's possible to adjust your body's energy flow and influence organ function, paving the way for enhanced healing and overall well-being (Oleson, 2014).

Acupuncture is often used in conjunction with other TCM practices, such as herbal medicine, cupping therapy, and tai chi, to provide a comprehensive treatment plan. It can be tailored to your specific needs, considering your physical, emotional, and environmental factors.

How You Can Go About It?

Consult with a Licensed Practitioner: Seek out a certified acupuncture practitioner with experience relevant to your health concerns. A skilled practitioner will ensure safe and effective treatment.

Be Open and Communicative: During your consultation, be honest and open about your health history, lifestyle, and any symptoms you're experiencing. This information will help your practitioner tailor the treatment to your specific needs.

Commit to a Treatment Plan: Acupuncture often requires multiple sessions to achieve desired results. Commit to the treatment plan recommended by your practitioner to fully experience the benefits.

Combine with Other Holistic Practices: Enhance the effects of acupuncture by integrating other holistic practices such as herbal medicine, proper nutrition, and physical activities like yoga or tai chi.

Yoga

From ancient India, yoga is a deeply holistic practice that revitalizes your mind, body, and spirit. It melds physical poses (asanas), controlled breathing (pranayama), and meditation (dhyana) to foster balance and harmony both within yourself and with the surrounding world. Yoga transcends the boundaries of mere physical activity, charting a course towards inner peace, resilience, and enduring vitality (Woodyard, 2011).

Yoga's comprehensive approach to wellness renders it a powerful tool for bolstering physical health, mental clarity, and emotional steadiness. Yoga offers a multitude of health benefits, including enhanced flexibility, strength, balance, and heart health. Research indicates that yoga is known to diminish stress, anxiety, and depression symptoms, cultivating a feeling of well-being and satisfaction (Ross & Thomas, 2010).

It plays a pivotal role in sustaining ageless vitality, nurturing your physical health, mental equilibrium, and emotional toughness. Studies show that regular yoga practice can boost your heart health, lessen inflammation, and aid in the healthy aging process (Gowans et al., 2019). Moreover, yoga's focus on mindfulness and being present in the moment cultivates a positive life perspective, significantly improving your quality of life and longevity.

How You Can Go About It?

Start with Gentle Practices: Begin your yoga journey with gentle practices suitable for your fitness level. Yoga styles like hatha or Iyengar are great for beginners, focusing on foundational postures and alignment.

Create a Consistent Routine: Dedicate a specific time each day for your yoga practice. Even 15-20 minutes can be beneficial. Consistency is key to experiencing yoga's transformative effects.

Incorporate Mindfulness and Meditation: Enhance your practice by incorporating mindfulness and meditation. Spend a few minutes at the beginning or end of your practice focusing on your breath or engaging in guided meditation to deepen the mind-body connection.

Attend Classes or Use Online Resources: Join a yoga class to receive guidance from experienced instructors, or utilize online resources and apps for practice at home. This can provide structure and variety to your practice.

Listen to Your Body: Yoga is about tuning into your body's needs and limits. Modify postures as needed and use props to support your practice without strain.

By adding yoga to your daily life, you're choosing a comprehensive path to wellness that nurtures your body, mind, and spirit. This paves the way for a lifetime filled with health and timeless vitality. Regular yoga practice will lay down the groundwork for a life that's balanced, healthy, and full of vibrancy, no matter your age.

Immune Boosting Habits: Strengthening your Natural Defence Mechanisms

Your immune system is your body's foremost shield against infections and diseases. It's a sophisticated alliance of cells, tissues, and organs, united in their purpose to guard your body. Their chief role is to recognize and neutralize invaders like bacteria, viruses, and any foreign entities that breach your body's defenses, as well as to eradicate them. Having a strong immune system is pivotal for sustaining your overall health and zest for life. It's your personal guardian that allows you to fend off infections, lessen the severity of allergies, and lower the likelihood of chronic conditions such as autoimmune disorders and cancer. Nurturing your immune system translates into bolstering your body's innate capability to combat diseases, paving the way for a rich healthy life.

Actionable Habits for Developing a Healthy Immune System

Maintain a Balanced Diet: A diet rich in fruits, vegetables, whole grains, lean proteins, and healthy fats can provide essential nutrients that support immune function. Foods high in vitamin C (oranges, strawberries, bell peppers), vitamin E (almonds, sunflower seeds), and zinc (beans, nuts, seafood) are particularly beneficial (Childs et al., 2019).

Regular Physical Activity: Moderate exercise can bolster the immune system by promoting good circulation, which allows immune cells to move through the body more effectively. Aim for at least 150 minutes of moderate aerobic activity or 75 minutes of vigorous activity each week, combined with muscle-strengthening exercises on two or more days (Nieman & Wentz, 2019).

Adequate Sleep: Ensuring sufficient sleep each night allows the immune system to fight off infections. Adults should aim for 7-9 hours per night. Poor sleep quality can make you more susceptible to sickness (Besedovsky et al., 2019).

Stress Management: Chronic stress can weaken the immune system, making it less effective at fighting infections. Techniques such as mindfulness, meditation, and yoga can help manage stress levels (Dhabhar, 2014).

Stay Hydrated: Hydration doesn't directly protect you from germs and viruses, but preventing dehydration is important for overall health. Dehydration can cause headaches and hinder your physical performance, focus, mood, digestion, and heart and kidney function. These complications can increase your susceptibility to illness (Popkin et al., 2010).

Limit Alcohol Consumption and Avoid Smoking: Both alcohol and smoking can negatively impact immune health, making it harder for your body to defend itself against infections (Sarkar et al., 2015).

Adopting habits that boost your immune function shores up your defenses. It also elevates your overall health, laying the groundwork for a lifestyle marked by robustness, vitality, and endurance.

Other Holistic Health Approaches - An Introduction

Holistic health approaches offer a broad spectrum of practices dedicated to treating you—your body, mind, and spirit—as a whole rather than merely addressing disease symptoms. Alongside yoga, meditation, acupuncture, and mindfulness, let's explore other holistic health methods:

Ayurveda: Hailing from India over 5,000 years ago, Ayurveda stands as one of the planet's most ancient holistic healing systems. It operates on the principle that your health and wellness hinge on a harmonious balance between your mind, body, and spirit. Ayurveda promotes a lifestyle that includes diet, herbal treatments, massage, meditation, and breathing exercises to sustain or regain health (Yadav & Agarwal, 2024).

Naturopathy: Emerged from integrating traditional practices and 19th-century European healthcare approaches. Naturopathy emphasizes natural remedies and your body's intrinsic healing and maintenance capabilities. It encompasses a variety of therapies such as herbal medicine, massage, homeopathy, acupuncture, physical activity, and nutritional advice (Fleming & Gutknecht, 2010).

Traditional Chinese Medicine (TCM): Traditional Chinese medicine, or TCM as it's called, is an age-old healthcare system based on clinical experience. Beyond acupuncture, TCM extends to herbal remedies, cupping therapy, tai chi, and qi gong. It's founded on the concept of qi (vital energy). It seeks to restore health through a blend of mind and body practices (Matos, Machado, Monteiro, & Greten, 2021).

Homeopathy: Homeopathy is a widely used form of complementary and alternative medicine (CAM). This medical system believes your body can heal itself. It employs minuscule quantities of natural substances, like plants and minerals, to trigger the healing process (Rehman & Ahmad , 2017).

Reiki: Originating in Japan, Reiki is a form of energy healing where practitioners use palm healing or hands-on healing to channel a "universal energy" to you, aiming to promote emotional or physical healing (Deutsch & Anderson, 2008).

Aromatherapy: Aromatherapy is a widely used complementary therapy that's growing in popularity. This practice uses essential oils for their medicinal properties to enhance both your physical and emotional well-being, supporting the health of your body, mind, and spirit. It uses scented oils extracted from plants to treat medical conditions such as anxiety, pain, depression, and insomnia (Farrar & Farrar, 2020).

Chiropractic Care: This method focuses on your musculoskeletal and nervous systems. Additionally, exercise and nutritional guidance might be included in the treatment plan. Chiropractors adjust the spine or other body parts to correct alignment issues, relieve pain, and foster your body's natural healing abilities (Coughlin, 2002).

Reflexology: This technique is grounded in the idea that specific zones and reflex areas on your feet, hands, and ears correspond to different body organs and systems. Stimulating these points can positively affect your health. Studies suggest reflexology sessions can influence the brain, triggering brainwave patterns similar to those experienced during sleep (Whatley, Perkins, & Samuel, 2022).

Biofeedback: Biofeedback is a technique designed to teach you control over your body's involuntary physiological processes, such as heart rate, muscle tension, and blood pressure. It is also used to improve overall health and wellness through stress management training. You learn to make conscious adjustments to enhance your health using sensors that provide feedback about your body (Frank, Khorshid, Kiffer, McKee, & Moravec, 2010).

Each of these holistic health practices brings its own unique benefits and pathways to wellness, underscoring the incredible capacity of your body to heal and maintain equilibrium.

What's Next?

I hope the life-changing power of weaving mindfulness practices, detoxification routines, and holistic healing methods into your everyday life made sense to you. These approaches do wonders for your physical health and for your mental and emotional wellness, setting the stage for a life brimming with ageless vitality.

We looked into the complex relationship between diet, environment, and mental health, learning how enhancing each area can lift your quality of life and foster longevity. Highlight of this chapter? Well, true longevity isn't just about increasing the number of years in your life but enriching those years with health, happiness, and fulfillment.

Remember, venturing into a vibrant, rewarding life doesn't hinge on making sweeping changes overnight. It's the small, consistent steps you take now that pave the way for significant health and wellness gains down the line. By embracing these practices, you step into each day with purpose and happiness, playing an active role in your journey toward long-lasting vitality.

As you move forward to Chapter 4, you'll build on the solid groundwork laid out before, focusing on how the social atmosphere you cultivate plays a crucial role in your well-being. I'll explore how joining clubs or groups that match your interests, participating in community service, and nurturing rich, diverse connections with family and friends can boost your health and joy. Stick around as I shine the light on the importance of not only caring for yourself but also building relationships that uplift and support you. Engaging with your community and cherishing the bonds you form, will help you create a supportive backdrop that enhances your personal wellness journey and contributes to the collective health of those around you.

CHAPTER 4

Creating A Supportive Environment

"There is no exercise better for the heart than reaching down and lifting people up."

-John Andres Holmes

This timeless adage eloquently sets the stage for Chapter 4, where you will explore the essence of cultivating a supportive environment. As Holmes suggests, nurturing and elevating others is not only a noble endeavor but also a necessary exercise for our hearts and souls. This chapter delves into how creating supportive spaces—both in our communities and our environments—plays a pivotal role in achieving a life of vitality and fulfillment.

As you begin flipping through the pages of this chapter, you'll discover the transformative power of nurturing deep, meaningful relationships that enhance your life and those around you. By diving into community service and valuing the connections with family and friends, you'll learn practical ways to create a strong support network that helps you navigate life's ups and downs. Additionally, I'll explore how you can incorporate ergonomics into your living spaces to boost comfort, safety, and well-being. I'll share insights on crafting a home that meets your physical requirements, calms your soul, and sparks your creativity.

Later, you will see the focus shift to reducing digital distractions to reclaim your mental clarity and strengthen your real-world connections. This section is packed with actionable tips for managing your digital life, ensuring that technology enhances your life rather than controls it. As you go into this chapter, remember that the environment you create—both in your social circles and physical spaces—plays a crucial role in your quest for a healthier, more joyful life. Embrace the principle of uplifting others, recognizing that by doing so, you lift yourself as well.

Building a Thriving Community Connection: Fostering Relationships that Nurture your Soul

In your search for a fulfilling life, the relationships that feed your soul are like lighthouses, guiding you through the serene and stormy seas of existence. These connections, rooted in deep understanding, mutual respect, and a shared feeling of belonging, offer more than companionship. They nurture your well-being, invigorate your spirit, and light up your journey. They are crucial to your survival, shaping your experiences, influencing your viewpoints, and responding to your innermost desires for love and acceptance.

As social beings by nature, these soulful connections lay the foundation of your life, providing a haven of support and comprehension essential for your emotional and psychological health. Such ties are important; they knit the strands of your social being, possessing the capacity to elevate, mend, and motivate. Beyond the immediate happiness and solace they bring, these relationships are essential for enduring vitality— they act as a shield against stress, boost your mental health, and create a nurturing space for you to flourish. By valuing and nurturing these deep bonds, you not only enhance your own life but also contribute to the health of your community, sending waves of positivity that reach well beyond your sphere. They play a significant role in your well-being, with studies showing that strong social ties can lead to enduring vitality and even slow down the aging process by lowering stress, improving mental health, and boosting longevity (Holt-Lunstad, Smith, & Layton, 2010).

However, it's essential to recognize that not all relationships positively affect our lives. Engaging with people who drain your energy without reciprocating—often referred to as "energy vampires"—can have detrimental effects on your mental and physical health. Being mindful of the quality of your relationships is crucial. It's okay to distance yourself from those who do not support your well-being. In cases where these relationships are with family members, setting clear boundaries is a healthy way to protect your emotional space while maintaining necessary ties. Building a tribe of like-minded individuals who uplift and support you can replace negative social interactions with positive ones, enhancing your life's quality.

How to Build Thriving Community Connections?

Building thriving community connections requires intentional effort and a willingness to step outside one's comfort zone. It's about creating and nurturing relationships that go beyond the superficial, fostering bonds that genuinely enrich our lives and the lives of others. Here's a deeper dive into how you can cultivate such connections:

Join Clubs or Societies Aligning with Your Interests

Finding a group that resonates with your passions or hobbies is a fantastic way to meet like-minded individuals. Whether it's a book club, a gardening society, or a sports team, these communities offer a space for shared experiences and mutual understanding. Participation in such communities has been linked to enhanced mental well-being, satisfaction, and a sense of belonging (Stebbins, 2007). The key is active participation; don't just attend meetings or events passively. Engage in discussions, volunteer for roles that excite you, and contribute your ideas. Active participation in groups that share your interests can lead to meaningful relationships, offering emotional and psychological benefits.

Engage in Community Service Projects

Volunteering connects you with people who share a common goal of making a positive impact. Whether it's helping at a local food bank, participating in environmental clean-up efforts, or teaching skills to younger generations, community service projects offer a sense of purpose and collective achievement. Studies have shown that engaging in community service can improve mental health, increase life satisfaction, and foster a sense of social connectedness (Post, 2005). These activities benefit those in need and create a bond among volunteers forged through the shared experience of giving back. Volunteering has been linked to numerous health benefits, including improved mental health and increased life satisfaction. It fosters a sense of belonging and contributes to a supportive community network (Piliavin, J. A., & Siegl, E., 2007).

Reach Out Frequently to Family and Friends

In our fast-paced, technology-driven lives, it's all too easy to let meaningful relationships drift into the background. While texting and messaging are convenient ways to stay in touch, consciously engaging more deeply can have profound effects. Consider picking up the phone for a call or arranging face-to-face meetups whenever possible. Voice conversations and in-person interactions can be much more powerful and meaningful, allowing for a richer exchange of emotions and stronger connections. These consistent interactions strengthen bonds and ensure your relationships continue growing and evolving. Remember, it's not about grand gestures; the regular, small acts of connection build a solid foundation of trust and mutual support. Studies have indicated that quality relationships with family and friends are associated with greater happiness and longevity (Diener, E., & Seligman, M. E. P., 2002).

Embrace Diversity in Friendships

Cultivating friendships with people from different ages, cultures, and backgrounds can profoundly enrich your life. These relationships open your eyes to new perspectives, experiences, and ways of thinking. These varied connections can also offer unique insights and wisdom, enhancing your worldview (Antonucci, Ajrouch, & Birditt, 2014). Research also suggests friendships across different cultures and backgrounds can enhance personal growth and social inclusion (Williams, D. R., & Mohammed, S. A., 2009). Make an effort to be open and inclusive, actively seeking opportunities to connect with individuals with different views of the world. Ask questions, listen actively, and share your own experiences. Diversity in friendships broadens your horizons and fosters a community that values inclusivity and mutual respect.

In building these connections, remember that the quality of relationships far outweighs quantity. Deep, meaningful interactions and shared experiences foster a sense of community that nourishes the soul and contributes to a vibrant, fulfilling life. Building thriving community connections is a dynamic process that requires time, patience, and genuine interest in others. By embracing these strategies, you can foster a relationship that supports and nurtures your soul. This network, in turn, fosters a profound sense of community and belonging.

Designing an Age-Friendly Home Environment: Implementing Ergonomics in Everyday Spaces

At its core, Ergonomics, is the study of designing products, systems, and spaces to fit the people who use them. The concept aims to foster environments that bolster human well-being and performance while reducing strain or injury risk. Regarding your home, ergonomics focuses on enhancing the efficiency and comfort of your daily tasks. This approach ensures activities are tailored to fit your unique needs and abilities, particularly as you grow older.

Taking a cue from the visionary architect Le Corbusier, who once said,

"A house is a machine for living in,"

Rather than considering living spaces as scenery, we can

proactively design them as dynamic ecosystems that promote holistic well-being and optimize vitality. To transform your home into a true haven of timeless vitality, you can rely on the insights of ergonomics. This science harmonizes you with your living spaces.

Applying ergonomics in your home means thoughtfully analyzing how spaces and items are utilized and the interaction between you and your surroundings. This approach includes everything from arranging furniture to selecting appliances to ensure usability, accessibility, and safety. For instance, height-adjustable chairs can support various activities and body types, alleviating the risk of back pain or discomfort. Likewise, touch-free faucets offer ease for those with limited dexterity, enhancing both independence and cleanliness.

Vitality and Healthier Living Through Ergonomic Design

The importance of an ergonomically designed home extends beyond mere physical comfort. It plays a critical role in promoting vitality and healthier living. By reducing the physical strain associated with daily tasks, ergonomically designed environments can help preserve energy, reduce the risk of falls and injuries, and enhance overall quality of life. This is particularly vital as we age, ensuring our homes continue to support our independence and well-being.

Moreover, an ergonomic approach to home design can have significant mental and emotional benefits. A well-organized and thoughtfully designed space can reduce stress, improve mood, and contribute to a sense of control and satisfaction. This holistic improvement in well-being is essential for maintaining ageless vitality, as it supports the physical and psychological aspects of health.

In conclusion, by adopting the principles of ergonomics in our living spaces, you can honor Le Corbusier's vision of the home as a machine for living—a machine designed to support, nurture, and enhance our lives at every age. Implementing ergonomic solutions in our homes paves the way for a life of comfort, independence, and vitality, allowing you to thrive in environments that truly understand and meet your needs. Considering various practical enhancements that can make a significant difference in ensuring safety, comfort, and functionality is crucial. Let's have a look at how you can optimize your space to make it work like a well-oiled machine;

Install Grab Bars in Bathrooms: Grab bars near the toilet, shower, and bathtub areas provide necessary support, reducing the risk of slips and falls in wet areas. They are essential for maintaining balance and stability.

Use Non-slip Mats: Place non-slip mats in the bathroom, kitchen, and other areas prone to getting wet. This simple addition can prevent falls and provide extra safety in high-risk zones. Additionally, consider using anti-fatigue mats in areas where you spend a lot of time standing, such as in front of the kitchen sink or your workbench. These mats are designed to reduce fatigue in legs and feet caused by standing for prolonged periods on hard surfaces. Not only do they help in preventing slips, but they also provide cushioning support, enhancing comfort and reducing strain on the body.

Ensure Good Lighting, Especially Along Stairways: Adequate lighting is crucial for preventing accidents and ensuring easy navigation through the home. Pay special attention to stairways, hallways, and entryways, installing bright, easily accessible light fixtures.

Optimize Storage Spaces: Arrange storage spaces to minimize the need to reach high or bend low. Consider pull-out shelves, drawer organizers, and wall-mounted storage solutions to keep items within easy reach.

Choose Lever-style Door Handles: Lever-style door handles are more accessible to operate than traditional knobs, especially for people with arthritis or limited hand strength. This simple change can significantly enhance accessibility throughout the home.

Adjust Countertop Heights: If possible, adjust countertop heights to comfortably accommodate seated or standing positions. Variable heights can cater to different tasks and individual needs, promoting ergonomic postures during cooking or washing dishes.

Incorporate Ample Seating Areas: Ensure there are sufficient and varied seating options that offer proper support and comfort. Consider chairs with armrests and adjustable features to cater to different comfort needs.

Automate Where Possible: Invest in smart home technologies that automate lighting, heating, and security systems. Automation can reduce the need for physical interaction with devices, making daily routines more manageable.

Select Easy-to-use Appliances: When choosing appliances, prioritize models with intuitive controls, transparent displays, and features that enhance usability, such as front-loading washing machines or refrigerators with eye-level storage. Also, pay attention to the height at which appliances are installed. For instance, placing microwaves at a low height requires bending down, which can be inconvenient and physically straining over time. This simple adjustment makes your kitchen environment safer and more user-friendly.

Create Clear Pathways: Keep pathways within the home clear of obstacles and clutter. Wide, unobstructed walkways reduce the risk of tripping and make it easier to move around, especially for those using mobility aids.

These thoughtful considerations ensure that your environment adapts to your evolving needs, promoting a life of comfort and dignity at any age. Integrate these ergonomic enhancements into your living space to create an age-friendly home that supports independence, safety, and well-being.

Digital Detoxification Strategies: Reducing Electronic Interference in Your Quest Towards Vitality

Albert Einstein once shared a concern that deeply echoes in today's digital era:

"I fear the day when technology surpasses human interaction; we will have a generation of idiots."

This warning highlights the critical need to keep our relationship with technology in check. As you aim for timeless vitality, it's crucial to evaluate the influence of digital devices on your well-being and adopt measures to limit their potential adverse effects.

A digital detox is a period of time when you step away from electronic gadgets like smartphones, computers, and tablets. Its primary purpose is to lessen stress and enhance real-life connections without the interference of digital distractions. This practice has become increasingly indispensable as screen time permeates our daily lives, possibly leading to detrimental impacts on both mental and physical health.

The Role of Digital Detox in Promoting Vitality and Health

The relentless flow of notifications, emails, and social media alerts can lead to digital overwhelm, affecting your stress levels, sleep quality, and overall happiness. Research indicates that too much screen time can foster sedentary lifestyles, disturb your sleep, and heighten anxiety and depression (Twenge & Campbell, 2018). In contrast, a digital detox can help restore equilibrium, spur more physical activity, strengthen social bonds, and boost mental health. These are essential for sustaining vitality and embracing a healthful life.

Incorporating digital detox strategies into your life is critical to cultivating a lifestyle that upholds lasting health and vitality.

Establishing tech boundaries allows you to regain time for physical exercise, enrich in-person relationships, and indulge in mindfulness practices. This holistic approach ultimately enhances your quality of life. Moreover, cutting down screen time, especially before sleep, can improve sleep quality, aiding your body's healing mechanisms and bolstering your overall well-being (Chang, Aeschbach, Duffy, & Czeisler, 2015). In today's increasingly connected world, where the pervasive presence of technology can significantly impact our well-being. Implementing practical steps to manage and reduce digital consumption can foster healthier lifestyles. This, in turn, improves relationships and enhances overall vitality. Here are some strategies for you to consider:

Set Screen-Free Hours: Establish specific times during the day when all electronic devices are turned off, especially during meals and at least one hour before bedtime. This can help improve sleep quality and encourage meaningful family interactions (Chang, Aeschbach, Duffy, & Czeisler, 2015).

Use Device Usage Tracking Apps: Applications such as "Screen Time" on iOS and "Digital Wellbeing" on Android can help monitor and limit your daily screen time, providing insights into your digital habits and encouraging more conscious use of technology.

Designate Tech-Free Zones at Home: Create areas in your home where electronic devices are not allowed, such as bedrooms and dining areas. This promotes healthier sleep hygiene and fosters a space for uninterrupted personal or family time.

Implement a "Phone Bowl" Habit: Establish a family routine where everyone places their phones in a designated bowl or charging station in a common area, such as the kitchen, by a specific time each evening, e.g., 8 PM. This habit helps to reduce evening screen time and encourages family members to engage in other activities.

Switch Devices to Airplane Mode: Activating airplane mode on your devices during designated screen-free hours or while working on important tasks can minimize distractions and improve focus and productivity.

Reduce WiFi and Blue Light Exposure: To mitigate the potential impacts of WiFi and blue light exposure:

- Invest in blue light-blocking glasses to wear during screen time, especially during the evening, to help reduce eye strain and prevent disruption of sleep cycles.
- Install software like f.lux on computers and mobile devices, which adjusts the screen's color temperature according to the time of day, reducing blue light exposure in the evening. Some devices offer this as an inbuilt feature named Night Mode.
- Place salt lamps near modems or workspaces, as some believe they can neutralize electromagnetic radiation (though scientific evidence supporting this claim is limited).
- Turn off the WiFi modem at night to minimize electromagnetic field (EMF) exposure during sleep.
- Consider using Tesla plates or EMF harmonizers to potentially reduce the effects of electromagnetic radiation, however, it's important to note that scientific research supporting the efficacy of these devices is currently limited.

Schedule Unplugged Periods: Allocate certain times of the day or week to disconnect from all digital devices to enjoy offline activities.

Prioritize In-Person Connections: Make a conscious effort to engage in face-to-face interactions, which will enhance the quality of your relationships.

Engage in Regular Digital Detox Days: Dedicate one day a week (or a month) to a complete digital detox, where you refrain from using all digital devices. Use this time to reconnect with offline activities you enjoy, such as reading, hiking, or spending time in nature.

Incorporating these digital detox strategies can significantly improve physical and mental health, paving the way for a life characterized by vitality and connection. Let's heed Einstein's warning and embrace a balanced approach to technology, ensuring it enhances rather than detracts from our pursuit of ageless vitality.

Understanding Deeper Issues

If you notice that despite trying various digital detox strategies, you're still heavily leaning on technology, it might signal deeper issues that need expert attention. Sometimes, excessive screen time is a way to cope with deeper psychological or emotional challenges, like anxiety, depression, or other mental health conditions. It could also hint at underlying problems with self-esteem, social isolation, or difficulties in handling stress and emotions.

Anxiety and Depression: Research increasingly links too much screen time with higher levels of anxiety and depression. For some, constant online presence might worsen anxiety symptoms, while for others, the perfect lives depicted on social media can trigger feelings of depression.

Social Isolation: Digital platforms offer a semblance of connection, but depending too much on them for socializing can lead to real-world isolation, diminishing direct human interactions and the forging of meaningful bonds.

Stress and Emotional Management: Using digital devices as your primary way to deal with stress or to sidestep uncomfortable emotions can halt the development of more effective coping strategies. This, in turn, can trap you in a cycle of avoidance and heightened stress.

Seeking Professional Help

Knowing when to seek help is of utmost importance for your well-being. Reaching out for professional guidance is a sign of strength and a proactive measure towards health and vitality. Mental health experts can offer the support and tools you need to manage your tech use, tackle any root issues, and find healthier ways to cope.

Therapy: Approaches like cognitive-behavioral therapy (CBT) and counseling can be especially useful in tackling the psychological dimensions of tech overuse, helping you find other ways to manage stress, anxiety, and depression.

Support Groups: Participating in support groups, whether in-person or online, can give you a sense of belonging and insights from people who are dealing with similar issues.

Digital Wellness Programs: Some experts focus on digital wellness, providing tailored programs to help you control tech overuse.

It's essential—and okay—to ask for help if you're struggling with technology dependency. This step can lead to a healthier balance with digital devices, boosting your overall well-being and paving the way to a more satisfying, engaged life.

What's Next?

As Chapter 4 ends, you've traversed the enriching path of building a supportive environment that fosters your well-being and propels you toward a lifelong vitality. So, we talked about building strong social networks, creating comfy and useful living spaces, and finding a good balance with tech. These things all work together to help you live your best life! These insights highlight an important lesson: the ambiance you live in, the depth of your connections, and your engagement with technology are all integral to your quest for longevity.

By adopting the belief that your home should be a sanctuary designed to uphold your well-being at every turn, you need to step beyond traditional architectural boundaries into a realm where every nook, every piece of furniture, and even the silence from digital clamor adds to your vitality. This vision, drawing on the wisdom of both Le Corbusier and Einstein, serves as a gentle reminder that while technology and modern conveniences hold their value, they should never detract from the essential human experiences and interactions that nourish your soul and ignite your spirit.

As we step into the next chapter, you're poised to tackle the common health challenges of aging with grace. With the insights gained from Chapter 4, you're now more prepared to see these challenges not as inevitable fears but as parts of life that you can manage and positively influence through lifestyle adaptations, resilience, and mindfulness. From gracefully managing chronic conditions to maintaining mental sharpness and managing discomfort, the next chapter is set to provide practical advice and wisdom to empower you to view aging not just as a natural progression but as an avenue for personal development, learning, and enriching life.

Continue this journey with me as I uncover how today's choices—fueled by a harmonious home, the warmth of genuine connections, and the judicious use of technology—can significantly shape your health, happiness, and longevity in the years ahead. The quest for timeless vitality is far from over, promising more insights and strategies to illuminate your way to living fully at any age.

CHAPTER 5

Tackling Common Health Challenges While Aging

"Once you have turned eighty, it's important to have the right sort of wrinkles. Even more important though is to start laughing early enough to spend more time laughing than frowning. If your wrinkles point upward, you will look happy instead of merely old."

- Margareta Magnusson

This reflection by Margareta encapsulates the essence of aging gracefully—not just living to a ripe old age but doing so with joy, resilience, and vitality. As you venture into Chapter 5, I will guide you through addressing the inevitable health challenges of aging, not as daunting barriers as chances to reaffirm our dedication to wellness and vibrant living.

Aging is a shared journey accompanied by its unique trials. Still, it also brings unmatched opportunities for growth, wisdom, and satisfaction. This chapter will dive into the essential strategies and knowledge needed to manage chronic diseases, navigate mobility concerns, and maintain robust mental health as we age. From adopting lifestyle changes that bolster your physical well-being to learning pain management techniques that increase your comfort,

I will aim to nurture a quality life where each added year is a testament to living fully and with intention.

Next, we'll delve into the crucial topic of brain health. We'll explore scientifically grounded practices that can significantly reduce our risk of cognitive decline and boost brain function. By incorporating those strategies into our daily routine, we can keep our minds as agile and vibrant as our spirits. The goal is to approach these later years not with trepidation but with confidence, equipped with the knowledge and tools to navigate the complexities of aging. Let this chapter serve as a beacon of light, guiding you through the challenges while celebrating the incredible potential for joy, health, and vitality at every stage of life. Join me as I embark on this transformative journey. My goal isn't simply adding years to our lives; it's about strategically infusing every moment with life, laughter, and the kind of wrinkles that speak of a well-lived life.

Common Chronic Diseases and Lifestyle Changes

Managing chronic diseases is integral to sustaining health and vitality as we age. Chronic conditions such as diabetes, heart disease, and arthritis pose significant challenges to maintaining an active lifestyle. However, evidence suggests that adopting specific lifestyle changes can be crucial in managing and, in some cases, improving these conditions (Elmhurst, 2018).

Diabetes

Dietary Modifications: A balanced diet is crucial for managing blood glucose levels. The Diabetes Prevention Program (DPP) study demonstrated that diet modifications, including increased intake of fruits, vegetables, and whole grains while reducing fat and calorie intake, significantly reduced the risk of developing type 2 diabetes by 58% over 2.8 years compared to placebo (Knowler et al., 2002).

Physical Activity: Regular physical activity improves insulin sensitivity and helps control blood glucose levels. A meta-analysis by Umpierre et al. (2011) found that structured exercise interventions of more than 150 minutes per week were associated with an average A1C decrease of 0.89% in individuals with type 2 diabetes.

Weight Management: Maintaining a healthy weight is essential for managing diabetes. Even modest weight loss can improve insulin resistance and blood glucose levels and reduce the risk of developing type 2 diabetes. The Look AHEAD (Action for Health in Diabetes) trial showed that participants who underwent an intensive lifestyle intervention focusing on weight loss through dietary changes and physical activity improved glycemic control and reduced the need for diabetes medications (Look AHEAD Research Group, 2013).

Stress Management: Stress can affect blood glucose levels. Techniques such as mindfulness, yoga, and regular exercise can help reduce stress and positively affect blood glucose control (Hartmann et al., 2012).

Sleep Quality: Adequate sleep is essential for blood glucose regulation. Poor sleep can affect insulin sensitivity and potentially lead to weight gain, exacerbating diabetes symptoms. Research indicates that improving sleep quality can benefit glucose control and overall health in individuals with diabetes (Knutson & Van Cauter, 2008).

Heart Disease

Heart disease encompasses a range of conditions affecting the heart, including coronary artery disease, arrhythmias, and congenital heart defects. It remains one of the leading causes of morbidity and mortality worldwide. Still, a significant portion of heart disease risk is modifiable through lifestyle changes. Factors such as high blood pressure, high cholesterol, smoking, and a sedentary lifestyle increase the risk (Lopez, Ballard, & Jan, 2023).

Dietary Modifications: Adopting heart-healthy diets, such as the Mediterranean diet or the Dietary Approaches to Stop Hypertension (DASH) diet, has significantly reduced cardiovascular disease risk (Lopez, Ballard, & Jan, 2023). These diets emphasize fruits, vegetables, whole grains, lean protein, and healthy fats. A seminal study by Estruch et al. (2013) on the Mediterranean diet supplemented with extra-virgin olive oil or nuts found a substantial reduction in the risk of major cardiovascular events among individuals.

Physical Activity: Regular exercise is a cornerstone of heart disease prevention and management. It helps improve cardiovascular fitness, lowers blood pressure, reduces LDL cholesterol, and enhances insulin sensitivity. The American Heart Association recommends at least 150 minutes of moderate-intensity aerobic activity or 75 minutes of vigorous aerobic activity per week (American Heart Association, 2024). A meta-analysis by Sattelmair et al. (2011) concluded that higher levels of physical activity were associated with a 14% to 26% reduction in coronary heart disease risk.

Smoking Cessation: Smoking is a significant risk factor for heart disease. Quitting smoking can rapidly decrease the risk of heart disease and stroke, with cardiovascular risk approaching that of never-smokers within a few years. Critchley and Capewell (2003) highlighted that smoking cessation is associated with a significant reduction in coronary heart disease risk, among other health benefits.

Weight Management: Maintaining a healthy weight through diet and exercise can significantly reduce the risk of developing heart disease. Obesity is a risk factor for coronary artery disease, mainly due to its association with high blood pressure, dyslipidemia, and diabetes. The Look AHEAD study demonstrated that weight loss could improve cardiovascular disease risk factors in individuals with type 2 diabetes (Look AHEAD Research Group, 2013).

Stress Management: Chronic stress has been linked to an increased risk of heart disease. Techniques such as mindfulness, meditation, and stress reduction strategies can help mitigate this risk. A review by Boyle et al. (2017) suggests that mindfulness-based interventions may reduce blood pressure, a key risk factor for heart disease.

Arthritis

Arthritis encompasses a range of joint diseases and conditions characterized by inflammation in one or more joints, leading to pain and stiffness that typically worsen with age. The most common types are osteoarthritis (OA), which affects joint cartilage and underlying bone, and rheumatoid arthritis (RA), an autoimmune disorder affecting the lining of joints. Effective management of arthritis often involves a combination of medical treatment and lifestyle modifications (Senthelal, Li, Ardeshirzadeh, & Thomas, 2023).

Exercise: Regular physical activity is essential for managing arthritis. It helps maintain joint flexibility, strengthens the muscles around the joints, and improves overall physical function. A systematic review by Uthman et al. (2013) highlighted the effectiveness of exercise in reducing pain and improving physical function in people with OA without exacerbating pain or disease severity.

Diet: While no specific diet cures arthritis, certain dietary patterns can help fight inflammation, strengthen bones, and boost the immune system. The Mediterranean diet, rich in fruits, vegetables, whole grains, and omega-3 fatty acids, has reduced inflammation and pain in individuals with RA (Sköldstam et al., 2003).

Weight Management: For individuals with arthritis, maintaining a healthy weight is crucial. Excess weight puts additional pressure on weight-bearing joints, such as the hips and knees, worsening OA symptoms. Weight loss can significantly improve pain, function, and quality of life (Christensen et al., 2007).

Stress Management: Chronic stress can trigger arthritis flare-ups and amplify pain. Mindfulness, yoga, and other stress-reduction techniques can help manage stress and reduce the overall impact of arthritis on quality of life (Zautra et al., 2008).

Avoiding Joint Strain: Modifying activities to reduce strain on affected joints is important. Assistive devices, adaptive equipment, and learning proper body mechanics can help protect joints during daily activities (Pendergast, 2023).

Chronic Respiratory Diseases

Chronic respiratory diseases, including chronic obstructive pulmonary disease (COPD) and asthma, are prevalent conditions that significantly impact individuals' health, quality of life, and longevity. These diseases are characterized by long-term respiratory symptoms and airflow limitation, often linked to an abnormal inflammatory response in the lungs and airways. Effective management of chronic respiratory diseases involves a combination of medical treatment and lifestyle changes. Lifestyle modifications can reduce symptoms, improve lung function, and enhance overall well-being (Siddharthan et al., 2019).

Smoking Cessation: Smoking is the leading cause of COPD and significantly exacerbates asthma symptoms. Quitting smoking can halt the progression of the disease and improve lung function. A landmark study, the Lung Health Study, demonstrated that smoking cessation significantly slows the rate of decline in lung function in individuals with mild to moderate COPD (Anthonisen et al., 1994).

Physical Activity: Regular exercise can improve respiratory muscle strength, enhance lung function, and increase exercise tolerance in individuals with chronic respiratory diseases. A systematic review by Geddes et al. (2019) found that pulmonary rehabilitation, including exercise training, significantly improves the quality of life and reduces hospital admissions for COPD patients.

Avoiding Respiratory Irritants: Minimizing exposure to air pollution, occupational dust and chemicals, and indoor pollutants can reduce symptom flare-ups. For individuals with asthma, avoiding allergens is also crucial to managing the condition (Siddharthan et al., 2019).

Healthy Diet: Although research directly linking diet to respiratory disease outcomes is evolving, some studies suggest that a diet rich in antioxidants (found in fruits and vegetables) may protect lung function. A study by Hanson et al. (2013) indicated that dietary intake of certain nutrients, including vitamins C and E, was associated with improved lung function in individuals with COPD.

Hypertension

Hypertension, commonly known as high blood pressure, is a prevalent condition where the long-term force of the blood against artery walls is high enough that it may eventually cause health problems, such as heart disease. It's often referred to as a "silent killer" due to its minimal symptoms despite its capability to lead to serious cardiovascular complications. Lifestyle modifications play a critical role in preventing and managing hypertension. It can significantly reduce your risk of hypertension by up to 15%. These changes can significantly lower blood pressure levels, reduce cardiovascular disease risk, and minimize the need for medication (Iqbal & Jamal, 2023).

Dietary Approaches: The Dietary Approaches to Stop Hypertension (DASH) diet is specifically designed to combat high blood pressure. It emphasizes the intake of fruits, vegetables, whole grains, and lean proteins while reducing the consumption of salt, red meat, sweets, and sugary beverages. A landmark study demonstrated that the DASH diet effectively lowers blood pressure in individuals with and without hypertension (Appel et al., 1997).

Physical Activity: Regular physical exercise, such as 150 minutes of moderate-intensity aerobic activity per week, can lower blood pressure and improve heart health (American Heart Association, 2024). A comprehensive analysis has shown that aerobic exercise reduces systolic blood pressure in patients with hypertension (Cornelissen & Smart, 2013).

Weight Management: Maintaining a healthy weight is crucial for controlling blood pressure. Weight loss can lead to significant reductions in blood pressure and is especially effective when combined with exercise (Neter et al., 2003).

Reducing Sodium Intake: Lowering salt intake can decrease blood pressure levels. A systematic review and meta-analysis highlighted the importance of reducing sodium consumption in managing hypertension (He & MacGregor, 2002).

Limiting Alcohol and Cessation of Smoking: Moderating alcohol consumption and quitting smoking can further improve blood pressure control and overall cardiovascular health (Husain, Ansari, & Ferder, 2014).

Obesity

Obesity is a chronic medical condition caused by accumulating high body fat, specifically adipose tissue. It is a complex disease caused by genetics and lifestyle factors. Behaviors include dietary patterns, physical inactivity, medication use, and other exposures. Additional contributing factors include the food and physical activity environment, education and skills, and food marketing and promotion. Obesity is a significant contributor to severe health conditions, including heart disease, diabetes, and arthritis, significantly impacting an individual's quality of life (Panuganti, Nguyen, & Kshirsagar, 2023).

Lifestyle changes are fundamental in managing obesity effectively. Research has consistently shown that weight loss achieved through dietary modifications and increased physical activity can significantly reduce the risk of developing obesity-related conditions. The Look AHEAD (Action for Health in Diabetes) trial is a notable study that provided strong evidence that intensive lifestyle intervention focusing on weight loss through exercise and diet modification reduces obesity and related cardiovascular risk factors in individuals with type 2 diabetes (Look AHEAD Research Group, 2013).

Balanced Diet: A customized dietary plan with regular weight monitoring is crucial for optimal weight loss. Low-calorie diets are generally recommended, with options for either carbohydrate restriction or fat restriction. While low-carbohydrate diets may lead to faster weight loss than low-fat diets. It's important to emphasize and support an individual's ability to stick with their chosen dietary plan (Panuganti, Nguyen, & Kshirsagar, 2023).

Surgery: Surgery is an option for individuals with a very high BMI (40+) or a BMI of 35+ with serious weight-related health issues. Success hinges on post-surgical lifestyle changes and doctor follow-up. Standard procedures include adjustable gastric banding, Roux-en-Y gastric bypass (fastest weight loss), and sleeve gastrectomy. All surgeries carry risks, including infection, blood clots, and nutrient deficiencies (Stahl & Malhotra, 2023).

Regular Physical Activity: Physical activity increases your body's energy expenditure. Think of it like burning extra calories throughout the day. This creates a calorie deficit, meaning you burn more calories than you consume, which can lead to weight loss or help you maintain a healthy weight. Remember, a balanced diet is still crucial for overall weight management (Kim et al., 2017).

Behavioral Changes: For obesity, the USPSTF recommends referral to intensive behavior therapy programs. These programs can provide valuable support and equip individuals with tools for long-term weight management. Several effective approaches exist, including motivational interviewing, cognitive behavioral therapy (CBT), dialectical behavioral therapy (DBT), and interpersonal psychotherapy (IPT) (Panuganti, Nguyen, & Kshirsagar, 2023).

Mental Health Disorders

The World Health Organization emphasizes that mental and physical health are inseparable. Mental health disorders, including depression and anxiety, significantly impact quality of life and are linked to various chronic physical health conditions.

Lifestyle interventions, such as exercise, diet, and stress management, have significantly positively impacted mental health disorders (Njoku, 2022).

Exercise: Physical activity is highly beneficial for mental health. A meta-analysis by Schuch et al. (2016) found that exercise has a large and significant antidepressant effect in people with depression, including those with major depressive disorder. Regular physical activity can also reduce anxiety symptoms, improve mood, and boost self-esteem.

Diet: Nutritional psychiatry is an emerging field exploring the impact of diet on mental health. A study by Jacka et al. (2017) demonstrated that dietary improvements significantly reduced symptoms of depression, emphasizing the potential of diet as a strategy for managing mental health conditions.

Stress Management: Techniques such as mindfulness, meditation, and yoga have been shown to effectively reduce symptoms of anxiety and depression. A systematic review and meta-analysis by Goyal et al. (2014) highlighted that mindfulness meditation programs can lead to moderate reductions in psychological stress and anxiety.

Overcoming Mobility Issues & Improving Resilience

Overcoming mobility issues and enhancing resilience is crucial for maintaining quality of life, especially as you age. Mobility problems stem from various causes, including arthritis, back pain, or injuries. They can significantly impact daily activities and independence. However, through regular strength-building exercises and resilience training, individuals can improve muscle agility, enhance balance, and ensure their body functions like a well-oiled machine (National Institutes on Aging, 2020).

Strength-Building Exercises for Mobility

Strength-building exercises are essential for enhancing mobility and overall quality of life in older adults. These exercises help to increase muscle mass, improve balance, and reduce the risk of falls, which are common concerns as we age. Older adults can maintain and improve their independence and physical function by incorporating regular strength training into their routines (National Institutes on Aging, 2020).

Muscle Mass and Strength: As we age, we naturally lose muscle mass and strength, a condition known as sarcopenia. This loss can lead to decreased mobility, increased risk of falls, and a decrease in quality of life. Strength-building exercises counteract the effects of sarcopenia by stimulating muscle growth and enhancing muscular strength. Fiatarone et al. (1994) conducted a seminal study demonstrating that high-intensity resistance training significantly increased muscle strength, gait velocity, and stair-climbing power among frail residents of nursing homes aged 72 to 98.

Bone Health: Strength training is also beneficial for bone health, as it helps to increase bone density and reduce the risk of osteoporosis. A study by Zhao et al. (2015) found that resistance training positively affected bone mineral density in older adults, indicating its importance in preventing osteoporosis-related fractures.

Functional Mobility: Improved muscle strength and bone health directly contribute to better functional mobility, allowing older adults to perform daily activities more efficiently and with less effort. This includes tasks such as walking, climbing stairs, and carrying groceries. Liu and Latham (2009) reviewed multiple trials. They concluded that progressive resistance strength training improves the physical functioning of older adults, enhancing their ability to perform daily activities.

Recommended Strength-Building Exercises

Exercise Category	Specific Exercises	Benefits
Leg Presses and Squats	-Leg Press Machine -Bodyweight Squats -Goblet Squats	Targets major muscles of the legs, improving lower body strength and stability.
Upper Body Exercises	-Overhead Presses -Bicep Curls -Seated Rowing	Strengthens arms, shoulders, and back, contributing to better posture and upper body mobility.
Core Exercises	-Modified Planks -Seated Abdominal Twists	Enhances core stability, crucial for balance and fall prevention.

Improving Resilience

Resilience plays a critical role in promoting health and mitigating the negative impacts of chronic diseases as you age. Resilience refers to the capacity to recover quickly from difficulties; it's about bouncing back from adversity and learning from the experience to emerge stronger and more resourceful. For older adults, resilience is not only about overcoming mobility challenges but also about maintaining a positive outlook on life despite the changes that come with aging (Hassani, Izadi-Avanji, Rakhshan, & Majd, 2017).

Physical Activity: Regular exercise, including strength training and balance exercises, contributes significantly to physical resilience by enhancing muscle strength, flexibility, and overall mobility. A study by Sjösten and Kivelä (2006) highlights the positive effects of physical activity on resilience, demonstrating improvements in physical functioning and independence among older adults.

Social Connections: Strong social networks provide emotional support and a sense of belonging, which are critical components of resilience. Hawkley and Cacioppo (2010) discuss how social isolation can negatively impact health and resilience, emphasizing the importance of maintaining social connections for mental and emotional well-being.

Mindfulness and Stress Reduction: Mindfulness, meditation, yoga, and tai chi can help reduce stress and anxiety, promoting mental resilience. A review by Goyal et al. (2014) found that mindfulness meditation programs can improve psychological stress and well-being.

Healthy Lifestyle Choices: A balanced diet, adequate sleep, and avoiding harmful habits like smoking and excessive alcohol consumption contribute to physical health and resilience. Proper nutrition supports immune function and recovery, while good sleep hygiene is essential for cognitive function and emotional regulation (Hildon, Smith, Netuveli, & Blane, 2008).

Lifelong Learning: Engaging in new activities, learning new skills, and embracing hobbies can enhance cognitive resilience and provide a sense of achievement and purpose. For instance, learning a new language, taking up musical instruments, or exploring digital photography stimulates the brain and introduces novel challenges that keep the mind active. Similarly, hobbies such as gardening, chess, or volunteering also offer mental engagement and social interaction opportunities. A study by Hertzog et al. (2009) supports the concept of cognitive resilience, suggesting that engaging in mentally stimulating activities is associated with a lower risk of cognitive decline.

Adaptive Coping Strategies: Developing adaptive coping mechanisms to deal with change and adversity, such as problem-solving skills, seeking help when needed, and maintaining a positive outlook, is fundamental to resilience. Luthar et al. (2000) explore the role of adaptive coping in resilience, highlighting its importance in overcoming challenges. Resources like the American Psychological Association (APA) website provide accessible materials on coping strategies and resilience. Books on resilience and coping, workshops, and online courses can also offer valuable guidance on developing and enhancing these critical skills for navigating life's challenges.

Mental Health Care As You Age

As you journey through the complexities of aging, taking care of your mental health gains paramount importance, especially when it comes to tackling issues like depression, anxiety, and cognitive decline. Carl Jung's profound observation, "Who looks outside dreams; who looks inside awakes," highlights the critical role of self-reflection and active management of your mental well-being during this stage of your life.

The process of aging can bring about various emotional challenges, such as dealing with the loss of loved ones, transitioning into retirement, and adapting to changes in physical health, all of which can contribute to feelings of depression and anxiety. You must understand that reaching out for professional support in these times is a sign of strength, not a shortcoming. Connecting with therapists or counselors can offer invaluable support and strategies to navigate these emotions more effectively (National Institute of Mental Health, 2024).

Staying socially connected is crucial for mental well-being. Research by Holt-Lunstad, Smith, and Layton (2010) demonstrated the significant impact of social relationships on health outcomes, indicating that solid social bonds are associated with reduced mortality risk and various mental health issues. Social activities and maintaining close relationships can offer emotional support and a sense of belonging.

Participating in endorphin-releasing activities, such as regular exercise, has positively affected mood and mental health.

Physical activity can act as a natural antidepressant. A study by Schuch et al. (2016) found that exercise has a large and significant antidepressant effect in people with depression. Activities that bring joy and satisfaction, whether gardening, dancing, or walking, can significantly enhance mental health and quality of life.

Enhancing Brain Function & Preventing Cognitive Decline

Enhancing brain function and preventing cognitive decline are crucial aspects of aging healthily and maintaining quality of life. Just as physical exercise strengthens the body, mental exercises can fortify the brain, reducing the risk of cognitive decline (Yamasaki, 2023). Brain-stimulating activities are akin to exercising a muscle; the more it's worked, the stronger and more resilient it becomes.

Puzzles and Brain Games: Engaging in puzzles like crosswords, Sudoku, or brain games can significantly improve cognitive functions by challenging memory, problem-solving skills, and attention to detail. Notably, games such as bridge and mahjong, often played in groups, offer the added benefit of encouraging social interaction, which is crucial for mental health and cognitive resilience (Urwyler et al., 2023). Similarly, physically active games like squash or pickleball require physical coordination, strategic thinking, and planning, promoting both cognitive and social engagement. A study by Nouchi et al. (2013) found that playing brain-training games can improve cognitive functions, including executive functions and processing speed, in young adults. These activities' combined cognitive and social benefits underscore their value in maintaining cognitive health and fostering a sense of community and connection.

Reading and Continuous Learning: Regular and continuous learning activities stimulate the brain, enhance vocabulary, and improve empathy and understanding. They also contribute significantly to personal development at any age. Engaging in intellectually stimulating activities, including reading, is a journey of continuous personal growth, allowing individuals to evolve their perspectives, refine their character, and enhance their emotional intelligence. This process of lifelong persona development underscores the idea that one is always young enough to work on personal growth. Snowden et al. (2011) demonstrated that such engagement across the lifespan is associated with lower rates of Alzheimer's disease and dementia, highlighting the profound impact of intellectual and personal development activities on cognitive health and overall well-being.

Learning a New Language: Learning additional languages challenges the brain, improves cognitive flexibility, deters cognitive decline, and enhances problem-solving skills. A study by Bialystok et al. (2007) highlighted that bilingualism can delay the onset of dementia symptoms.

Brain Training Apps and Software: Digital platforms offer a variety of brain training exercises designed to enhance cognitive functions. These apps and games target memory, attention, flexibility, and problem-solving skills. Though research on their long-term benefits is ongoing, they provide a convenient and engaging way to stimulate the brain (Kable et al., 2017).

Cognitive decline is another concern for many older adults. However, engaging in mentally stimulating activities, lifelong learning, and brain training exercises can help maintain cognitive function. A review by Hertzog, Kramer, Wilson, and Lindenberger (2008) highlighted that cognitive engagement through various activities could contribute to cognitive resilience in aging, potentially delaying the onset of cognitive decline. It's essential to approach mental health care as an integral part of overall well-being, especially as one ages. This includes:

Regular Check-ups: Just as physical health is monitored, regular mental health check-ups can help identify and address issues early.

Mental Stimulation: Engaging in hobbies, learning new skills, and participating in community activities can keep the mind active.

Healthy Lifestyle Choices: A balanced diet, regular physical activity, and adequate sleep support mental health.

Adopting a lifestyle that incorporates mentally stimulating activities, physical exercise, a balanced diet rich in omega-3 fatty acids, antioxidants, and adequate sleep contributes significantly to brain health. Regular social interaction and a positive outlook on life support cognitive resilience.

Pain Management

Managing pain is a critical aspect of ensuring a comfortable aging experience. As individuals grow older, they may encounter various forms of age-related pain, such as arthritis, chronic joint pain, or muscular discomfort. Sometimes, chronic pain's impact goes beyond discomfort. It can limit mobility in daily activities. Additionally, it often creates mental health issues and sleep problems, worsening overall well-being (Reid, Eccleston, & Pillemer, 2015). Fortunately, numerous non-invasive techniques can effectively reduce discomfort and enhance the quality of life without relying solely on pharmaceutical interventions.

Non-Invasive Pain Management Techniques

Physiotherapy: Physiotherapy involves tailored exercise programs, manual therapy, and education on body mechanics. It plays a significant role in alleviating pain, improving mobility, and restoring physical function. A systematic review by Jansen et al. (2011) highlighted the effectiveness of physiotherapy in reducing pain and improving physical function in patients with knee osteoarthritis.

Acupuncture: Acupuncture, a traditional Chinese medicine technique involving the insertion of fine needles into specific points on the body, has effectively reduced various types of pain. In the study by Vickers et al. (2012) on acupuncture, they compared real acupuncture to two other groups: one group that got "fake" acupuncture (where needles didn't go into the usual acupuncture points or weren't inserted deeply) and another group that didn't get any acupuncture at all. They found that the real acupuncture did a better job at reducing chronic pain than either the fake acupuncture or doing nothing, showing that acupuncture has a genuine benefit in managing pain. This has been discussed in detail in Chapter 3; refer for more information.

Mind-Body Techniques: Yoga and tai chi combine physical postures, breathing exercises, and meditation to reduce pain, improve flexibility, and enhance mental well-being. A study by Wang et al. (2010) demonstrated that tai chi could reduce pain and improve physical function in individuals with knee osteoarthritis.

Heat and Cold Therapy: Applying heat or cold to affected areas can relieve pain and reduce inflammation. Heat therapy increases tissue metabolism and blood flow, relaxes muscles, and reduces pain. In contrast, cold therapy reduces blood flow and cell metabolism, numbing the pain. Self-administered heat and cold treatments are simple yet effective strategies for managing acute and chronic pain (Wang et al., 2022).

Massage Therapy: Massage therapy can reduce muscle tension, increase circulation, and promote relaxation, contributing to pain relief. A randomized controlled trial by Perlman et al. (2006) found that massage therapy significantly reduced pain, anxiety, and depression in individuals with advanced cancer, showcasing its benefits in pain management.

What's Next?

Gazing outward, one may chase illusions, yet we awaken to the wisdom and beauty of aging gracefully by turning inward. This journey of introspection, likening our bodies to well-tuned machines, highlighted the necessity of continual care and upkeep. I addressed some chronic illnesses and brain-boosting activities and outlined effective pain management methods.

You've seen firsthand the pivotal role that actively participating in your health and wellness plays.

Now, as you step into a new chapter, you enter a realm filled with the challenges and gifts of aging. This next chapter explores the subtle yet impactful transformations your body experiences, aiming to arm you with the knowledge, grace, and flexibility to embrace these changes. Acknowledging the evolution in your physical and emotional states and adjusting your lifestyle to uphold autonomy, dignity, and independence will go a long way for you.

You'll discover strategies that recognize these shifts and prepare you to tackle them with insight and anticipation. From navigating through the natural phases of menopause and andropause to planning for the financial realities of retirement, this chapter will fill you with wisdom that seeks to ensure a future where independence and dignity are preserved as you age.

Join me on this enlightening journey, as I continue to lay the groundwork of self-awareness and proactive engagement with our health. Delving into the nuanced aspects of aging gracefully, we seize the chance to redefine living fully at every life stage, making sure each day is approached with energy, intent, and a profound sense of personal achievement.

CHAPTER 6

Special Circumstances In
Aging Well

*"Beautiful young people are accidents of nature, but beautiful
old people are works of art."*

– Eleanor Roosevelt

In Chapter 6, we embark on a journey through the special circumstances of aging well. We'll explore the idea that beauty in our later years isn't just about genetics - it's a masterpiece crafted through our choices, resilience, and how we carry ourselves. It is here that Eleanor Roosevelt's insightful words resonate deeply, reminding us that youthful beauty happens by chance. Still, the elegance of age is meticulously crafted. This chapter invites you to sculpt your own narratives of aging, navigating the complexities of menopause and andropause. The focus will be on embracing the changes these phases bring while laying the groundwork for a life marked by autonomy, dignity, and well-being.

As you traverse the landscapes of menopause and andropause, seek to understand the hormonal shifts and navigate them with grace and knowledge. These transitions are not merely biological occurrences but gateways to renewed understanding and acceptance of our evolving selves. Exploring the nuances of these changes can uncover ways to adapt your lifestyle, ensuring that your later years are lived with vibrancy and autonomy.

Living independently for as long as possible becomes paramount as you age. This chapter provides insights into adapting our daily routines, homes, and mindsets to support a lifestyle that champions independence and dignity. From practical advice on making homes more age-friendly to embracing a mindset that sees opportunity in change, I aim to equip you with the tools needed for a fulfilling, independent life. Furthermore, planning for the retirement years extends beyond financial preparation; it encompasses a holistic approach to ensuring that this chapter of life is rich with purpose, connection, and personal growth.

Through understanding, adapting, and planning, you can embrace the beauty of becoming a beautiful older person — not by accident, but by design.

Menopause & Andropause: Navigating Hormonal Changes with Grace

Menopause and andropause represent significant hormonal changes that mark a new phase in the lives of women and men, respectively. Understanding these changes is crucial for developing effective strategies to manage symptoms and maintain quality of life. For women, menopause typically occurs in their late 40s to early 50s. It is characterized by the end of menstrual cycles, signaling the conclusion of the reproductive years. Andropause, often referred to as male menopause, affects men usually after the age of 50 and involves a gradual decline in testosterone levels, which can affect energy levels, mood, and libido (Martelli, Zingaretti, Salvio, Bracci, & Santarelli, 2021).

Education and preparation are pivotal in navigating these transitions with grace. By understanding the biological changes of menopause and andropause, individuals can better manage symptoms and mitigate their impact on daily life. Symptoms such as hot flashes, mood swings, and changes in sexual function can be addressed through lifestyle modifications, hormone therapy, and other treatments when approached with knowledge and proactive care (Rose & Whelan, 2017).

Biological Changes During Menopause

Hormonal Fluctuations: The most significant change during menopause is the reduced estrogen and progesterone levels. Estrogen plays a crucial role in regulating menstrual cycles. It also involves many other body functions, including bone density, skin temperature, and cholesterol levels. The decrease in estrogen levels is responsible for most of the symptoms associated with menopause (Santoro et al., 2015).

Vasomotor Symptoms: Hot flashes and night sweats are common vasomotor symptoms experienced during menopause. These symptoms are attributed to the body's adjustment to varying estrogen levels. They can significantly affect sleep quality and daily functioning (Avis et al., 2015).

Osteoporosis Risk: Estrogen helps protect bone density. Its decline during menopause accelerates bone loss, increasing the risk of osteoporosis and fractures. The Study of Women's Health Across the Nation (SWAN) has shown a marked increase in bone turnover and loss during the menopausal transition, underscoring the importance of bone health management during this period (Sowers et al., 2006).

Cardiovascular Changes: Menopause is associated with an increased risk of cardiovascular disease. Estrogen's protective effects on the arterial walls diminish, leading to increased risk factors such as higher LDL cholesterol and lower HDL cholesterol levels, contributing to a greater risk of heart disease (El Khoudary et al., 2015).

Managing Symptoms and Mitigating Risks

Hormone Replacement Therapy (HRT): HRT can be effective in alleviating menopausal symptoms and is considered for short-term relief from hot flashes and vaginal dryness. However, its use must be individualized due to associated risks (Rossouw et al., 2002).

Lifestyle Modifications: A diet rich in calcium and vitamin D, regular weight-bearing exercise, and smoking cessation are key strategies to mitigate bone loss and cardiovascular risk. Managing stress through relaxation techniques and maintaining social connections can help alleviate vasomotor symptoms (Guthrie et al., 2001; Greendale et al., 1999).

Regular Health Screenings: Regular checkups for bone density, cholesterol levels, and cardiovascular health are crucial for early detection and management of menopause-related health risks (Rostami-Moez et al., 2023).

Biological Changes During Andropause

Decreased Testosterone: Testosterone levels decrease by about 1% per year after age 30. Still, the more significant drops characterize andropause and can affect overall health (Harman et al., 2001).

Reduced Muscle Mass and Strength: Lower testosterone levels contribute to decreased muscle mass and strength, impacting physical function and increasing the risk of falls (Baumgartner et al., 1999).

Increased Body Fat: Testosterone helps regulate fat distribution, so lower levels can increase body fat, particularly around the abdomen (Decaroli & Rochira, 2017).

Bone Density: Testosterone plays a role in bone metabolism; reduced levels can lead to decreased bone density and an increased risk of osteoporosis (Amin et al., 2000).

Emotional and Cognitive Impact: Andropause can lead to mood swings, irritability, depression, and cognitive changes, impacting quality of life (Moffat et al., 2002).

Strategies to Manage Symptoms

Lifestyle Adjustments: Many studies have found that different types of exercise, including cardio, strength training, and high-intensity interval training (HIIT), can boost testosterone levels and other hormones. This natural approach can also help reduce common andropause symptoms, such as obesity, weight gain, insulin resistance, and weak bones (Bhattacharya & Chatterjee, 2020).

Nutritional Considerations: A diet rich in calcium, vitamin D, and omega-3 fatty acids supports bone health and may help regulate body fat distribution.

Medical Interventions: Testosterone replacement therapy (TRT) can be considered for those with significantly low testosterone levels, following a thorough evaluation by a healthcare provider to weigh the benefits against potential risks.

Impact of Autonomy on Well-being

Adapting one's lifestyle to support independent living is essential during these changes. This adaptation might include regular physical activity, a balanced diet, and mental health support to manage stress and emotional well-being. Maintaining social connections and engaging in activities that promote cognitive health are also beneficial.

The importance of autonomy in seniors' well-being is well-documented. A study published in The Journal of Aging Studies underscores the positive relationship between maintaining independence, enhanced self-esteem, and overall happiness among seniors (Wister et al., 2016). This research validates that autonomy and a proactive approach to managing life's transitions can significantly contribute to a fulfilling and vibrant later life.

Last but not least, financial planning for retirement years gains added importance as one navigates through menopause and andropause. Preparing financially ensures that individuals can access necessary healthcare and support services, contributing to a sustained quality of life and independence.

Living Independently as You Age: Strategies to Maintain Autonomy and Dignity

Living independently as we age encapsulates more than the desire for autonomy; it's about preserving dignity and ensuring the quality of life amidst the inevitabilities of aging. As the global population ages—a phenomenon highlighted by the World Health Organization's projection that nearly 2 billion individuals will be 60 years or older by 2050—the need to address aging-related concerns proactively becomes paramount.

Strategies to Maintain Autonomy and Dignity

1. Home Modifications for Safety and Accessibility

This has been discussed in Chapter 4, and we've established that adapting living spaces to be more senior-friendly is essential for safe and independent living. This can include installing safety rails in bathrooms, ensuring homes are well-lit, using non-slip mats, and ensuring that daily necessities are within easy reach. Modifying homes to reduce fall risks can greatly enhance autonomy.

2. Embrace Technology for Independence

Technological advancements, such as personal emergency response systems, smart home devices, and telehealth services, can significantly support independent living. These technologies can offer peace of mind for seniors and their families, enabling older adults to stay connected and receive medical care remotely.

Personal Emergency Response Systems (PERS): Devices that allow users to call for help at the push of a button.

Smart Home Devices: Automated systems for lights, thermostats, and door locks can be controlled remotely, offering convenience and security.

Telehealth Services: Enable remote consultations with healthcare providers, making medical care more accessible.

Medication Management Apps: Help in tracking medication schedules and ensuring timely intake.

Adopting these technologies can help maintain independence while ensuring help is readily available when needed (Majumder, 2017).

3. Regular Health Check-ups and Preventive Care:

Staying on top of health through regular check-ups and preventive care is crucial for maintaining independence. Early detection and management of health issues can prevent them from escalating into more serious conditions that could impair one's ability to live autonomously.

Annual Physical Exams: To monitor vital health metrics and detect changes early.

Screenings: Regular screenings for conditions such as osteoporosis, cancer, and diabetes can catch diseases in their early stages.

Management of Chronic Conditions: Regularly monitor and manage existing chronic conditions to prevent complications. Consistent health maintenance can prevent minor issues from becoming severe, promoting a higher quality of life (Yardley, 2016).

4. Physical Activity and Healthy Eating

Maintaining a regimen of regular physical activity and a nutritious diet is paramount for aging individuals. Regular exercise strengthens your body, improves balance and mobility. It also benefits your mind by sharpening cognitive function and boosting emotional well-being. Activities such as walking, swimming, tai chi, and light resistance training (discussed in chapters 3 and 4) are particularly beneficial for aged adults, promoting cardiovascular health, muscle strength, and flexibility. A healthy diet plays a critical role in preventing and managing chronic diseases often associated with aging, such as heart disease, diabetes, and osteoporosis. Diets rich in fruits, vegetables, whole grains, lean proteins, and healthy fats, like the Mediterranean diet, have been shown to support healthy aging (Sofi et al., 2010).

5. Social Engagement and Community Involvement

As discussed in previous chapters, engagement in social and community activities is crucial for preserving mental and emotional health in older adults. Social interactions can reduce the risk of depression, cognitive decline, and even physical health problems. Participating in social groups, volunteer work, or community events provides opportunities for meaningful connections. It contributes to a sense of purpose and belonging. A study by Holt-Lunstad, Smith, and Layton (2010) highlighted the significance of social relationships on mortality risk, underscoring the importance of social engagement for longevity and well-being.

6. Financial Planning

Financial planning for retirement and potential healthcare needs is critical to maintaining independence and dignity in old age. Adequate financial preparation allows individuals to access necessary healthcare and support services, and maintain their standard of living without undue stress. This planning should include understanding and managing retirement savings, health insurance, long-term care insurance, and estate planning. It's advisable to consult with financial advisors to create a comprehensive financial plan that covers expected and unexpected costs in later life.

Preparing for the Golden Years Post-Retirement: A Fulfilling Life Beyond Work

Transitioning into retirement marks a significant shift from the structured routines of work to a period filled with potential for personal growth, relaxation, and exploration. Preparing for the golden years post-retirement is about crafting a fulfilling life beyond the confines of professional responsibilities. This preparation extends beyond financial security to encompass health, wellness, and personal happiness. It's a time to envision and implement a lifestyle that aligns with one's deepest values and desires, ensuring these years are not just spent but are rich with purpose and joy.

Embarking on this journey requires thoughtful planning and proactive measures. It's an opportunity to reflect on what truly matters and how to achieve it, considering the inevitable changes that come with aging. Understanding the physical transformations your body will undergo, maintaining your health through regular check-ups, and adapting your living environment for safety and comfort are foundational steps. These actions empower you to embrace retirement with enthusiasm and peace of mind.

Retirement opens a new chapter where the focus shifts from external achievements to internal fulfillment. It's a period for rediscovering passions, cultivating new interests, and strengthening connections with family and friends. By planning wisely and embracing the changes that come with aging, you can ensure that your golden years are not merely a continuation of what was but a vibrant beginning to what can be.

1. Educate Yourself About Hormonal Changes During Midlife

Understanding the hormonal changes that occur during midlife, such as menopause and andropause, is essential for navigating the physical and emotional transitions that accompany aging. Education on these topics can demystify the symptoms and challenges during these periods, enabling individuals to seek appropriate care and lifestyle adjustments. Knowledge about these changes fosters better dialogue with healthcare providers, ensuring personalized and effective management strategies.

2. Maintain Regular Health Checkups

Regular health checkups become increasingly vital as we age. These visits allow for the early detection and management of age-related health issues, such as cardiovascular diseases, diabetes, and osteoporosis, ensuring that they don't evolve into more severe conditions that could impair independence. Furthermore, consistent engagement with healthcare professionals provides an opportunity to adjust health management plans in response to the evolving needs of your body. This preventative approach optimizes your health and well-being, maximizing your ability to remain active and engaged throughout your retired life.

3. Start Financial Planning Early

Financial security is a cornerstone of a worry-free retirement. Starting your financial planning early can allow you to enjoy your retired life without financial stress. This involves saving consistently, investing wisely, and planning for unexpected healthcare costs. Seeking advice from a financial planner can help you navigate pensions, savings, and investments, ensuring you have a steady income stream to support your lifestyle and any medical needs that may arise (Lusardi & Mitchell, 2007).

4. Stay Physically Active and Socially Engaged

Maintaining an active lifestyle and staying engaged with your community is vital for physical and mental health. Regular exercise helps manage chronic conditions, improves mobility, and increases overall well-being. Additionally, staying connected with friends, family, and community activities can fend off loneliness, depression, and common challenges in later life. Social engagement and physical activity are linked to improved cognitive function and a lower risk of health decline, underscoring their importance in a fulfilling post-retirement life (Colcombe & Kramer, 2003; Holt-Lunstad, Smith, & Layton, 2010).

5. Have an Interest, Purpose, or Hobby to Stay Inspired and Lit Up

Finding a purpose or pursuing hobbies that ignite your passion can significantly enhance the quality of your retirement years. Whether gardening, painting, volunteering, or learning a new skill, engaging in activities that bring joy and fulfillment can provide a sense of accomplishment and identity beyond work. Research suggests that having a sense of purpose is associated with better physical health, reduced disease risk, and increased longevity (Boyle, Barnes, Buchman, & Bennett, 2009).

Integrating these strategies into your retirement life can ensure a balanced and enriching post-work life. Financial security, physical health, social connections, and personal fulfillment are all pillars of a satisfying and dignified retirement, enabling you to explore, grow, and enjoy life to the fullest.

What's Next?

By now, it's clear how crucial proactive steps are on your path to aging with elegance and grace. In a world where the number of older adults is rapidly increasing, preparing for the nuances of our later years is not just beneficial for you—it's a necessity for society. This chapter empowers you to manage the transitions of menopause and andropause. It equips you with strategies to make the most of your retirement life. You can build a future filled with independence, dignity, and satisfaction with your gained tools.

Yet, the journey into aging continues to unfold, inviting you to look forward to the future of longevity. Our exploration continues beyond understanding and adapting to changes within and around us. As you gaze toward what's next, a thrilling concept emerges, highlighted by groundbreaking research and technological advancements ready to reshape our understanding of aging. The upcoming and final chapter draws us into the world of anti-aging research, where scientists are decoding the secrets of our biological clocks, and technology opens new doors for health monitoring and improvement.

Envision a world where the limits of longevity are constantly extended, where each innovation offers a peek into a future filled with promise. In this future, aging is not just slowed but enhanced, empowered, and reimagined. Come along as I explore what the future holds, discovering the latest trends and tools set to revolutionize how we age, making sure our later years are not just longer but filled with unmatched vitality and well-being.

CHAPTER 7

The Future Of Longevity

"To continue to work, to continue to love what you do, is certainly a contributing element to one's longevity and health."
- John Williams

This is the final chapter, and you're about to dive into the exciting possibilities that lie ahead in extending the quality and length of our lives. The anti-aging research and health technology field is promising, offering new ways to boost our well-being and longevity. John Williams's wise words highlight the importance of continuing to work and love what you do, shining a light on our path. Persisting in your endeavors and cherishing your passions undeniably plays a significant role in enhancing both your lifespan and overall well-being. They echo the truth that passion, purpose, and engaging in what we love are not merely life's pleasures but essential ingredients for our health and longevity.

This chapter reveals the latest breakthroughs in anti-aging research aimed at decoding the secrets of aging at the cellular level, potentially transforming how we age. You'll learn about scientific progress designed to add years to life and ensure those years are healthy and vibrant. Moreover, you'll step into a future where technology significantly influences health monitoring and improvement. Wearable gadgets, intelligent health systems, and tailored medicine are revolutionizing healthcare, making it more proactive, personalized, and preventive than ever. These innovations empower you to take control of your health like never before, with instant access to data and interventions that can profoundly influence longevity.

Dive into cutting-edge anti-aging research and advancements in health monitoring. This chapter will ignite your enthusiasm for a future where aging is an exciting chapter, not a dreaded one.

Picture a future where the duration of our lives equals the quality of our health and vitality, where our continued engagement in work and passions enriches our lives, leading us towards a brighter, more enduring tomorrow.

Emerging Trends in Anti-Aging Research

Senescence

Scientists are on a mission to understand aging better! They're working hard to figure out how our bodies age and how to slow it down. This could mean living longer and feeling healthier for even more years. One such mechanism is cellular senescence, a condition in which cells cease to divide and begin to accumulate, losing their function and contributing to the deterioration associated with aging. This accumulation of senescent cells leads to increased inflammation and tissue damage, significantly accelerating aging. Senolytics represent a pioneering category of drugs to combat aging by targeting senescent cells. These cells, which have ceased to divide but do not die as they should, accumulate with age and contribute to various age-related diseases and the overall decline in bodily functions. By selectively eliminating these cells, senolytics offer a promising approach to extend lifespan and enhance the quality of life during aging (Kirkland & Tchkonia, 2020).

Mechanism of Action

Senolytics selectively induce apoptosis, or programmed cell death, in senescent cells. Unlike traditional therapies that may affect both healthy and senescent cells, senolytics are designed to spare normal cells, targeting only the senescent ones that contribute to aging and disease (Kirkland & Tchkonia, 2017).

Research and Development

The concept of senolytics emerged from the discovery that senescent cells express specific pathways that protect them from apoptosis. Researchers have developed senolytic agents capable of clearing senescent cells from tissues by identifying and targeting these pathways. This breakthrough has significant implications for aging research, offering a novel approach to delay or prevent age-related conditions (Zhu et al., 2017).

Potential Benefits of Senolytics

Senolytics potential benefits are vast and hold transformative promise for the field of aging and geriatric medicine. Recent advancements in senolytic drugs, which target and eliminate senescent cells, offer a revolutionary approach to aging. These drugs have the potential to significantly extend the health span, which is the duration of life spent in good health. This could lead to a fundamental transformation in managing and potentially preventing age-related diseases (Lorenzo, Torrance, & Haynes, 2023).

1. **Delaying Aging and Extending Healthspan**

   One of the most compelling prospects of senolytics is their potential to delay the biological processes of aging, extending the period of healthy life. By clearing senescent cells, which accumulate with age and contribute to declining physical and cognitive functions, senolytics could significantly slow aging markers and extend the health span (Xu et al., 2018).

2. **Prevention and Mitigation of Age-Related Diseases**

   Senescent cells have been implicated in a wide range of age-related diseases, including cardiovascular diseases, diabetes, neurodegenerative disorders, and various forms of cancer. Senolytics offers a novel approach to treating these conditions and potentially preventing them by addressing one of their root causes. Reducing senescent cell burden could decrease inflammation and improve tissue function, thereby lowering the incidence and severity of age-related diseases (Childs et al., 2017).

3. Improvement in Physical Function

The accumulation of senescent cells contributes to the loss of muscle strength, joint function, and overall mobility associated with aging. By eliminating these cells, senolytics could improve physical function and mobility in seniors, enhancing their ability to perform daily activities and maintain independence. Studies in animal models have shown improved physical performance following senolytic treatment, suggesting similar benefits might be achievable in humans (Justice et al., 2019).

4. Enhanced Tissue Repair and Regeneration

Senescent cells contribute to aging and disease and interfere with the body's natural repair mechanisms. Senolytics could rejuvenate the body's ability to repair and regenerate tissues by removing the cells hindering these processes. This has implications for wound healing, recovery from injuries, and even the reversal of tissue degeneration, offering a new avenue for regenerative medicine (Tchkonia et al., 2013).

5. Cognitive Benefits

There is growing evidence to suggest that senolytics may also have cognitive benefits, potentially preventing or delaying the onset of neurodegenerative diseases such as Alzheimer's and Parkinson's. By reducing senescent cell load and associated inflammation in the brain. Senolytics could help preserve cognitive function and prevent the mental decline typically seen in aging (Bussian et al., 2018).

Challenges in Senolytic Research and Application

While senolytics offer promising avenues for extending health span and mitigating the effects of aging, several challenges and future directions need careful consideration to realize their full potential.

Selective Targeting and Side Effects

One of the primary challenges lies in ensuring that senolytics selectively target only senescent cells without affecting healthy cells. Achieving this specificity is crucial to minimizing potential side effects and ensuring the safety of these therapies. Further research is needed to refine the selectivity of senolytic agents and understand their long-term impacts on the body's normal functioning (Kirkland & Tchkonia, 2020).

Identifying the Optimal Timing for Intervention

Determining the most effective timing for senolytic intervention poses another challenge. Early intervention may prevent the accumulation of senescent cells, but the long-term effects of such an approach remain unknown. Conversely, later intervention may require more aggressive treatment to clear accumulated senescent cells, which could carry higher risks or reduced efficacy (Childs et al., 2017).

Understanding the Role of Senescence in Cancer and Tissue Regeneration

While senescence is associated with aging and age-related diseases, it also protects against cancer by preventing the proliferation of damaged cells. Additionally, senescent cells are involved in wound healing and tissue regeneration. Balancing the removal of harmful senescent cells while preserving these beneficial effects is a complex challenge that requires further elucidation (Campisi, 2013).

Future Perspectives on Senolytic Research

While the potential benefits of senolytics are profound, it is essential to note that research is still in its early stages, particularly concerning human applications. Ongoing clinical trials and further studies are necessary to fully understand the implications, optimal dosages, and long-term effects of senolytics on human health and longevity.

Combination Therapies

Combining senolytics with other therapeutic strategies, such as immunotherapy or regenerative medicine, could enhance their effectiveness. Combining treatments may provide synergistic benefits, addressing multiple aspects of aging and age-related diseases. (Xu et al., 2018).

Personalized Medicine Approaches

Given the variability in how individuals age and the complexity of biological aging processes, personalized medicine approaches to senolytic therapy may be necessary. Tailoring treatments to individual genetic, environmental, and health profiles could maximize benefits while minimizing risks (Tchkonia et al., 2013).

Long-term Clinical Trials

Conducting long-term clinical trials in humans is essential to assess the efficacy, safety, and potential side effects of senolytic drugs. These trials will provide critical data needed to move senolytics from the laboratory to clinical use, offering insights into how these therapies impact human health and lifespan.

Senolytics are at the cutting edge of anti-aging research, offering hope for a future where we can live longer and healthier, with reduced burden from age-related diseases and an improved capacity for physical function and recovery. The exploration of senolytics stands as a beacon of hope in the quest to enhance our golden years in terms of longevity and the quality and vitality of life. Even though its path is fraught with challenges that necessitate careful, coordinated research efforts, the potential rewards for aging populations worldwide make overcoming these obstacles a compelling goal for the future of longevity science.

Telomeres

Telomeres, the repeating DNA sequences that cap the ends of chromosomes, serve as protective buffers during cell division, ensuring the integrity of genetic information. As cells replicate, telomeres shorten a process that is intricately linked to aging. The progressive shortening of telomeres limits the number of times a cell can divide, a phenomenon known as the "Hayflick limit." Once telomeres reach a critically short length, cells enter a state of senescence or programmed cell death, contributing to the aging process at the cellular level and the onset of age-related diseases. This relationship between telomere length and cellular aging has propelled scientists to explore extending telomeres, positing that such interventions could theoretically enable us to live longer, healthier lives (Shammas, 2011).

The Significance of Telomere Research in Longevity

Research has shown a correlation between telomere length and lifespan. Individuals with longer telomeres tend to have a lower risk of developing age-related diseases and a longer lifespan (Cawthon et al., 2003).

Link to Age-Related Diseases

Telomere length is closely associated with age-related diseases. Shorter telomeres have been linked to an increased risk of numerous conditions, including cardiovascular disease, diabetes, Alzheimer's disease, and various cancers. The connection between telomere length and these diseases underscores the potential of telomere research in developing interventions that could delay or prevent the onset of age-related conditions, thereby extending healthy lifespan (Blackburn et al., 2015).

Telomerase Activation: A Potential Anti-Aging Mechanism

The enzyme telomerase can add nucleotide sequences to the ends of telomeres, potentially counteracting telomere shortening. This discovery has led to a surge in research exploring telomerase activation as a strategy to extend telomere length and enhance cellular longevity. In various model organisms, increased telomerase activity has been shown to improve healthspan, delay aging, and even extend lifespan, offering a glimpse into the possibilities of harnessing this enzyme for anti-aging therapies (Bernardes de Jesus & Blasco, 2011).

Implications for Human Health and Longevity

The implications of telomere research for human health and longevity are profound. By understanding the mechanisms that govern telomere maintenance and developing strategies to protect or restore telomere length, scientists hope to devise interventions that can slow the aging process, reduce the incidence of age-related diseases, and improve the quality of life in later years. This includes pharmacological approaches, such as developing telomerase activators or telomere-protective compounds, and lifestyle interventions that may positively affect telomere length, such as diet, exercise, and stress reduction (Epel et al., 2004).

Emerging Research on Telomere Extension

One avenue of research focuses on activating the enzyme telomerase, which can extend and maintain telomere length. Studies have demonstrated that activating telomerase in cells can reverse some signs of aging and extend the lifespan of specific cell types (De Jesus et al., 2011).

Scientists are also exploring gene therapy techniques to deliver telomerase directly into cells, aiming to promote telomere elongation and combat cellular aging. This approach has shown promise in preclinical models for improving healthspan and combating age-associated issues (Bernardes de Jesus et al., 2012).

Challenges

Despite the exciting potential, telomere research faces challenges. Therefore, future research must carefully balance the benefits of telomere extension with the potential risks. Additionally, more studies are needed to translate findings from model organisms to humans and to develop safe, effective, and accessible anti-aging therapies based on telomere biology.

Understanding Telomere Dynamics

The relationship between telomere length, aging, and disease is complex and poorly understood. While short telomeres are associated with aging and age-related diseases, overly long telomeres can disrupt cellular function and stability. Research must continue to unravel these dynamics to identify therapeutic windows that balance benefits and risks (Armanios & Blackburn, 2012).

Cancer Risk

One of the most significant concerns associated with telomere extension is the increased risk of cancer. Telomerase, the enzyme responsible for extending telomeres, is often found in high levels in cancer cells, allowing them to divide indefinitely. Therefore, strategies to activate telomerase or extend telomeres must be cautiously approached to avoid inadvertently promoting tumorigenesis (Artandi & DePinho, 2010).

Individual Variability

Genetic, environmental, and lifestyle factors influence significant telomere length variability among individuals. This variability poses a challenge in developing universal telomere-based interventions. Tailored approaches considering individual differences may be necessary for effective and safe applications

(Blackburn et al., 2015).

Future Directions

Developing Safe Telomere Therapies

Future research must focus on creating safe, controlled methods for telomere extension that minimize the risk of adverse effects, including cancer. This may involve targeted delivery systems, temporal control of telomerase activation, or novel agents that can selectively lengthen telomeres without affecting cancer risk (Bernardes de Jesus & Blasco, 2016).

Comprehensive Biomarker Panels

Developing a comprehensive panel of biomarkers that includes telomere length and other indicators of biological aging could enhance our understanding of aging processes and the efficacy of anti-aging interventions. Such biomarkers would facilitate personalized medicine approaches to longevity, enabling interventions tailored to an individual's biological age and health status (Justice et al., 2018).

Ethical and Social Considerations

As telomere-based therapies advance, it will be crucial to address ethical, social, and accessibility issues. Questions about the equitable distribution of anti-aging therapies, the societal implications of extended lifespans, and the definition of healthy aging must be thoughtfully considered to ensure these advancements benefit society (Caplan, 2019).

Longitudinal and Diverse Population Studies

Long-term studies across diverse populations are essential to understanding the long-term effects of telomere extension and uncovering how genetic diversity and environmental factors influence telomere dynamics and aging. Such studies will provide invaluable insights into the universality of telomere-based interventions and their potential impacts across different population segments (Frenck et al., 2017).

In conclusion, telomere research stands at the forefront of the quest for understanding and extending human longevity. It offers a promising avenue for unraveling aging mysteries and developing interventions that could significantly impact health span and lifespan. As research advances, the hope is that insights from telomeres will lead to breakthroughs that enable people to lead longer, healthier lives.

Leverage Technology to Live Longer

Leveraging technology to live longer has become a fundamental aspect of today's health and wellness strategies. With an array of technological tools at your disposal, you now have unparalleled access to data and resources that can profoundly influence your health span and lifespan. This era of innovation offers you the tools to actively participate in enhancing your well-being, promising a future where living healthier and longer is not just a possibility but a reality within your grasp. These technologies range from wearable devices that track physical activity and heart rate to mobile applications designed for meditation, sleep improvement, and nutrition management. Their widespread adoption underscores a growing trend toward data-driven personalized health care.

The Role of Fitness Trackers

Physical Activity Monitoring: Fitness trackers encourage users to achieve daily step goals, engage in regular exercise, and monitor the intensity of their workouts. These devices help individuals maintain motivation and track progress over time by providing real-time feedback and historical data. Research indicates that using fitness trackers can significantly increase physical activity, improving cardiovascular health and weight management (Bravata et al., 2007).

Heart Rate Monitoring: Many fitness trackers include heart rate monitors that provide insights into cardiovascular health and exercise intensity. Monitoring heart rate during exercise helps users maintain the correct intensity for achieving fitness goals, while resting heart rate data can signal overall heart health and recovery status (Altini & Plews, 2021).

Sleep Tracking: Sleep is a critical component of health and longevity, and fitness trackers offer tools to analyze sleep patterns, including duration, quality, and sleep stages. This information can help users identify trends or issues with their sleep, guiding adjustments to improve sleep hygiene and overall health (Chinoy et al., 2021).

Nutritional Guidance: Meal planning and nutrition tracking apps provide users with the tools to monitor their dietary intake, set nutritional goals, and adhere to healthy eating habits. By tracking macronutrients, micronutrients, and caloric intake, individuals can make informed decisions about their diet, supporting weight management and chronic disease prevention (Franco et al., 2016).

In summary, fitness trackers and health apps represent a convergence of technology and health, empowering individuals with the knowledge and tools to manage and improve their health actively. As these technologies evolve, their potential to contribute to longevity and well-being will only increase, highlighting the importance of integrating digital health solutions into everyday life.

Telomere Testing Kits

Direct-to-consumer telomere testing kits, offered by companies like Elysium Health, have enabled individuals to gauge their biological age by assessing the length of their telomeres. This technological advancement provides a unique window into one's cellular health, allowing for targeted lifestyle adjustments and interventions. Although the interpretation and implications of telomere length measurements are complex and require further research, these kits represent a significant step towards personalized health and aging strategies (Aviv et al., 2011).

Personal Health Insights: Telomere testing gives individuals a unique glimpse into their biological aging process, which can be a powerful motivator for healthier lifestyle choices. Understanding one's biological age can prompt changes in diet, exercise, stress management, and other factors that positively influence telomere length and overall health.

Preventive Health Measures: By providing early warnings about potential aging-related health risks, telomere testing can encourage proactive measures to prevent or delay the onset of chronic diseases. Individuals with shorter telomeres for their age group might be more motivated to engage in preventive health practices and seek medical advice to address potential risks (Aviv et al., 2011).

It's crucial to approach these tests with an understanding of their limitations and the broader context of health and aging. As science advances, telomere testing may become an increasingly valuable tool in the quest for longevity, complemented by a holistic approach to health and wellness.

DNA Sequencing

DNA sequencing services, which have become increasingly accessible to the general public, offer profound insights into genetic makeup, predispositions to specific health conditions, and ancestral heritage. By analyzing one's DNA, these services can reveal a wealth of information, from genetic variants associated with disease risks to traits that might influence nutrition and exercise responses. This burgeoning field represents a significant leap forward in personalized medicine and preventive health care, empowering individuals with knowledge once limited to scientists and medical professionals.

DNA sequencing can identify genetic variants that increase the risk of developing certain diseases, such as breast cancer (BRCA1 and BRCA2 genes), heart disease, Alzheimer's, and type 2 diabetes. Early detection of these predispositions allows individuals to take proactive steps in consultation with healthcare professionals to mitigate these risks through lifestyle changes, regular screenings, and preventive therapies (Hernandez & Blazer, 2006). Nutrigenomics is the study of how genetics influence nutritional needs and responses to diet. Like nutrigenomics, pharmacogenomics examines how genetic differences affect an individual's drug response. DNA sequencing services can provide insights into how an individual's body might metabolize certain foods, their likelihood of lactose intolerance, or sensitivity to caffeine, guiding more personalized and effective dietary choices. It also helps predict which medications are likely most effective and which might cause adverse reactions, leading to more tailored and safer prescribing practices (Heather & Chain, 2016). While DNA sequencing services offer exciting possibilities for health and wellness, they also raise essential challenges and ethical considerations:

Accuracy and Interpretation: The accuracy of risk assessments provided by consumer DNA sequencing services can vary, and understanding the implications of genetic findings often requires professional interpretation. There's a risk of misinterpretation by consumers, leading to unnecessary anxiety or false reassurance.

Privacy and Data Security: The sensitive nature of genetic data necessitates stringent privacy protections. Users must know how their data is stored, used, and potentially shared, including the implications for insurance and employment.

Informed Decision-Making: Access to genetic information can lead to difficult decisions, particularly regarding diseases with no known cure or effective treatment. Genetic counseling can play a critical role in helping individuals understand their results and make informed decisions about their health care.

DNA sequencing services represent a pivotal development in personal health management, offering insights that can lead to more informed, personalized, and preventive health care strategies. As DNA sequencing technology advances, its integration into regular health care and preventive medicine is likely to deepen. Ongoing research aims to enhance the predictive power of genetic testing, expand its applications in personalized medicine, and address ethical, legal, and social implications. Collaboration between geneticists, clinicians, ethicists, and policymakers will be a defining factor in comprehending the future of DNA sequencing services to maximize benefits while minimizing risks.

Today, technology empowers individuals to control their health and longevity proactively. From wearable devices to genetic testing, the tools at our disposal enable personalized health management like never before. While technology offers innovative tools and services to enhance health and longevity, the most effective strategies for extending life quality remain rooted in simple lifestyle changes. Regular exercise, a balanced diet, adequate sleep, and stress management through mindfulness, meditation, and yoga practices are pivotal in enhancing lifespan and quality of life. These foundational elements of health are supported by a wealth of scientific research underscoring their benefits in promoting longevity and preventing chronic diseases (Matthews et al., 2017).

What's Next?

As I close the narrative on the groundbreaking explorations of longevity, I'm gently reminded by Mark Twain that age is a matter of mentality over reality. If it doesn't bother you, then it's insignificant. This whimsical yet profound adage encapsulates the essence of our journey towards understanding aging. The discoveries discussed in this chapter reveal a future not preordained but one that you can shape with mindful choices and innovative strides in science and technology.

I've tried to simplify the complexities of biological versus chronological age, learning that the clock ticks differently within our cells. This distinction is crucial, highlighting that longevity is less about the years in our life and more about the life in our years. The pioneering research into cellular interventions, such as the promising yet still nascent fields of telomere extension and senolytics, is a testament to humanity's quest to extend life and infuse it with quality and vitality. Technology, our steadfast companion in this quest, offers tools that empower us to take the helm of our health. From the intimate insights provided by DNA sequencing services to the daily guidance of fitness trackers and health apps, you're equipped more than ever to tailor your lifestyle to your unique health blueprint. These advancements are not just gadgets and data points but lanterns lighting the path to a personalized approach to health and longevity.

Yet, as we chart this course towards a future brimming with possibilities, we're reminded of the collective journey of aging as a global society. The demographic shift towards an older population by 2050, mirroring Jeanne Calment's extraordinary voyage to 122 years, underscores the urgency and importance of our endeavours in longevity research. The revelation that strong social connections can bolster lifespan by up to 50% weaves a narrative of interconnectedness, emphasizing that our longevity is deeply intertwined with the quality of our relationships and communities.

In this confluence of science, technology, and human experience, we stand at the cusp of the final chapter, poised to draw together the strands of knowledge and aspiration explored thus far. It's an unwritten chapter, inviting us to envision a future where the twilight years are not dimmed by decline but illuminated by wellness and wisdom.

As you step forward, carry the insights and inspirations from this journey, embracing the notion that the art of aging is not just in living longer but in living well.

GLOSSARY OF TERMS

Activities of Daily Living (ADLs): Routine activities people do every day without assistance, including eating, bathing, dressing, toileting, transferring (walking), and continence.

Adaptogens: Natural substances considered to help the body adapt to stress and to exert a normalizing effect upon bodily processes.

Antioxidants: Molecules that fight free radicals in the body, potentially reducing damage to cells and combating aging.

Autophagy: The body's way of cleaning out damaged cells to regenerate newer, healthier cells, contributing to cellular health and longevity.

Bone Density: A measure of the amount of minerals (mainly calcium and phosphorus) contained in a certain volume of bone, used in assessing the risk of osteoporosis.

Blue Zones: Regions of the world where people live significantly longer lives, often studied to understand factors contributing to longevity.

Body Mass Index (BMI): A measure of body fat based on height and weight that applies to adult men and women.

Biological Age: An estimate of an individual's age based on various biomarkers, rather than chronological time. It reflects the physical and functional condition of the body's systems.

Caloric Restriction: Reducing average daily caloric intake below what is typical or habitual, without malnutrition, which has been shown to extend lifespan in various organisms.

Cardiovascular Health: A general term referring to the health of the heart and blood vessels, crucial for longevity.

Cellular Senescence: The process by which cells cease to divide and grow, entering a state of permanent growth arrest without dying. Senescent cells contribute to aging and age-related diseases.

Chronological Age: The actual time that has elapsed from an individual's birth to the present day.

Cognitive Decline: The deterioration of intellectual functions such as memory, with advancing age or in neurodegenerative diseases.

Cognitive Reserve: The mind's resistance to damage of the brain; higher cognitive reserve is believed to help ward off cognitive decline.

Circadian Rhythms: Physical, mental, and behavioral changes that follow a 24-hour cycle, affecting sleep, hormone levels, body temperature, and other bodily functions, which are critical for health and longevity.

Detoxification: The physiological or medicinal removal of toxic substances from the human body, a concept often applied in the context of diet and lifestyle interventions aimed at promoting health.

DNA Methylation: A biochemical process influencing gene expression, with patterns changing as we age and serving as an indicator of biological age.

DNA Sequencing: The process of determining the precise order of nucleotides within a DNA molecule. It includes any method or technology used to determine the order of the four bases: adenine, guanine, cytosine, and thymine.

Epigenetics: The study of changes in organisms caused by modification of gene expression rather than alteration of the genetic code itself.

Exercise Physiology: The study of the acute responses and chronic adaptations to a wide range of physical exercise conditions.

Ergonomics: The study of people's efficiency in their working environment, often applied to creating age-friendly home and work spaces that promote health and prevent injury.

Fasting Mimicking Diet (FMD): A low-calorie, low-protein, low-carbohydrate, high-fat plan that mimics the effects of periodic fasting on the body.

Functional Food: Foods that have a potentially positive effect on health beyond basic nutrition, purported to promote specific health benefits.

Functional Independence: The ability to carry out activities of daily living without assistance, a key aspect of aging healthily and maintaining quality of life.

Free Radicals: Molecules with an unpaired electron that can cause oxidative stress by damaging cells, proteins, and DNA. The body naturally produces free radicals as a byproduct of metabolic processes, but excessive levels can contribute to aging and the development of chronic diseases. Gerontology: The study of aging and the problems of the aged.

Geroprotectors: Agents that aim to affect the root cause of aging and to increase life span through molecular and cellular mechanisms.

Glycation: A process where sugar in the bloodstream attaches to proteins, forming harmful new molecules called advanced glycation end-products (AGEs), implicated in aging and chronic diseases.

Health Literacy: The degree to which individuals have the capacity to obtain, process, and understand basic health information and services needed to make appropriate health decisions.

Holistic Health: A concept in medical practice upholding that all aspects of people's needs, psychological, physical, and social, should be taken into account and seen as a whole.

Hormesis: A process by which a low dose of a potentially harmful stressor (like exercise or fasting) can activate biological responses that protect and repair the body, improving health and longevity.

Immune Modulation: The process of modifying the immune system's response to various stimuli, which can be critical for reducing age-related decline in immune function.

Immunosenescence: The gradual deterioration of the immune system brought on by natural age advancement, affecting the body's ability to respond to infections and diseases.

Inflammation: A vital part of the body's immune response; chronic inflammation is linked to several age-related diseases.

Insulin Sensitivity: The sensitivity of cells to the hormone insulin, crucial for blood sugar management. Decreased sensitivity (resistance) is linked with aging and chronic diseases.

Intermittent Fasting: An eating pattern that cycles between periods of fasting and eating, with implications for weight management and healthspan.

Junk DNA: A colloquial term for regions of DNA that are noncoding, with ongoing research exploring their potential roles in aging and disease.

Kinesthetic Awareness: The ability to know where your body parts are in three-dimensional space, which can decline with age but can be improved with practices like yoga and tai chi.

Lean Body Mass: The mass of the body minus the fat (includes muscle, bone, water, and organs), important for metabolic health and longevity.

Lifespan: The length of time for which a person or organism lives.

Longevity Escape Velocity: The theoretical situation in which life expectancy is extended longer than the time that is passing, due to advances in anti-aging therapies.

Meditation: A practice where an individual uses a technique to focus their mind on a particular object, thought, or activity to achieve a mentally clear and emotionally calm state.

Metabolic Health: A state of having ideal levels of blood sugar, triglycerides, high-density lipoprotein (HDL) cholesterol, blood pressure, and waist circumference, without using medications.

Microbiome: The collection of all the genetic material within a microbiota (the entire collection of microorganisms in a specific niche, such as the human gut).

Mindfulness: The practice of being aware of the present moment, which can improve mental wellbeing and reduce stress.

Mindful Eating: The practice of being fully attentive to the experience of eating and drinking, both inside and outside the body, which can influence food choices and consumption patterns beneficial for longevity.

Mitochondrial Function: The performance of mitochondria, the powerhouse of the cell; mitochondrial dysfunction is a hallmark of aging.

Neuroplasticity: The brain's ability to reorganize itself by forming new neural connections throughout life, important for learning and recovery from brain injury.

Nutrient Density: Refers to the amount of nutrients a food contains in comparison to the number of calories. Food with a high nutrient density is rich in nutrients when compared to its calorie content.

Nutrigenomics: The study of the effects of foods and food constituents on gene expression.

Organic Foods: Foods produced using methods that do not involve modern synthetic inputs such as synthetic pesticides and chemical fertilizers, considered by some to be healthier and more sustainable.

Oxidative Stress: An imbalance between free radicals and antioxidants in the body, which can lead to cell and tissue damage.

Pharmacogenomics: The study of how genes affect a person's response to drugs. This relatively new field combines pharmacology (the science of drugs) and genomics (the study of genes and their functions) to develop effective, safe medications and doses tailored to a person's genetic makeup.

Physical Activity Guidelines: Recommendations for the amount and types of physical activity needed to maintain or improve overall health and reduce the risk of chronic diseases.

Polyphenols: Micronutrients with antioxidant activity found in many foods and beverages, including fruits, vegetables, tea, and wine, thought to extend lifespan.

Prebiotics: Non-digestible food ingredients that promote the growth of beneficial microorganisms in the intestines.

Probiotics: Live bacteria and yeasts beneficial for health, especially the digestive system.

Proteostasis: The regulation of the body's proteins, including their synthesis, folding, trafficking, and degradation; disruptions are linked with aging.

Psychosocial Factors: Psychological and social factors that influence mental health and wellbeing, important for healthy aging.

Quercetin: A flavonoid found in many fruits and vegetables, known for its antioxidant properties and potential health benefits, including anti-aging effects.

Resilience Training: Programs or strategies designed to enhance an individual's resilience or ability to bounce back from stress and adversity, important for mental health and well-being.

Resveratrol: A compound found in red wine and some plants, thought to have antioxidant properties and potential health benefits including anti-aging effects.

Senolytics: A class of drugs designed to selectively induce the death of senescent cells, aiming to improve healthspan and potentially extend lifespan by reducing the burden of these aging cells.

Sarcopenia: The loss of muscle mass, strength, and function that occurs with aging.

Senescence: The condition or process of deterioration with age; loss of a cell's power of division and growth.

Social Determinants of Health: Conditions in the environments in which people are born, live, learn, work, play, worship, and age that affect a wide range of health, functioning, and quality-of-life outcomes and risks.

Stem Cell Therapy: The use of stem cells to prevent or treat a disease or condition, with potential applications in anti-aging treatments.

Stress Management: Techniques and therapies aimed at controlling a person's levels of stress, especially chronic stress, for the purpose of improving everyday functioning.

Telomerase: An enzyme that adds nucleotide sequences to the ends of telomeres, potentially extending their length and influencing the aging process of the cell.

Telomeres: Protective caps located at the ends of chromosomes, which shorten with each cell division. Telomere length is associated with cellular aging and longevity.

Vascular Health: The health of the body's network of blood vessels, essential for overall health and longevity.

Vitamins and Minerals: Essential nutrients the body needs in small amounts to work properly and stay healthy, important for preventing disease and promoting longevity.

Wearable Technology: Electronic devices worn on the body as accessories or implants, which can monitor health and fitness data.

Whole Foods: Foods that are as close to their natural form as possible and not processed or refined, important for maintaining health and preventing disease.

Xerophagy: A form of fasting that involves a diet of dry foods, historically practiced for religious reasons but also studied for its potential health benefits.

Yogic Breathing: Controlled breathing practices that are a central part of yoga, believed to improve physical and mental well-being.

Zeaxanthin: A carotenoid alcohol found in many fruits and vegetables, known for its role in eye health and potential to protect against age-related macular degeneration.

ADDITIONAL RESOURCES

The Blue Zones: Secrets for Living Longer - Dan Buettner

Fast Like Girl: Dr Mindy Pelz

The Fast 800: Dr Michael Mosley

Ikigai: The Japanese Secret to a Long Happy Life - Hector Garcia

The Power of Now: Eckhart Tolle

How to Meet Your Self: Dr Nicole LePera

Letting Go: David R. Hawkins

www.mindvalley.com

Melanie Speers Gratitude Diary: www.givingthanks.co

The Ageing Brain: Timothy R Jennings

1. "The Resilience Factor" by Karen Reivich and Andrew Shatté: A book offering practical advice on developing resilience through seven key skills, including realistic optimism and emotional regulation.

2. "Bouncing Back: Rewiring Your Brain for Maximum Resilience and Well-Being" by Linda Graham: This book provides insights into how to recover from setbacks and thrive in the face of challenges.

3.Coursera and other online learning platforms: Look for courses on resilience, stress management, and psychological well-being to gain more structured knowledge.

REFERENCES

CHAPTER 1

Anton, S. D., Moehl, K., Donahoo, W. T., Marosi, K., Lee, S. A., Mainous, A. G., ... & Mattson, M. P. (2018). Flipping the Metabolic Switch: Understanding and Applying Health Benefits of Fasting. Obesity, 26(2), 254-268.

Benson, H., Wilcher, M., Greenberg, B., Huggins, E., & Ennis, M. (2000). Self-reported health and illness and the use of conventional and unconventional medicine and mind/body healing by Christian Scientists and others. Journal of Nervous and Mental Disease, 188(9), 589-596.

Black, D. S., O'Reilly, G. A., Olmstead, R., Breen, E. C., & Irwin, M. R. (2015). Mindfulness meditation and improvement in sleep quality and daytime impairment among older adults with sleep disturbances: A randomized clinical trial. JAMA Internal Medicine, 175(4), 494-501.

Boyce, P. R., Robertson, S. A., & Lockley, S. W. (2016). Effects of exposure to intermittent versus continuous red light on human circadian rhythms, melatonin suppression, and pupillary constriction. Physiology & Behavior, 164, 277-283.

Boyle, P. A., Barnes, L. L., Buchman, A. S., & Bennett, D. A. (2009). Purpose in life is associated with mortality among community-dwelling older persons. Psychosomatic Medicine, 71(5), 574-579.

Buettner, D. (2009). The blue zones: 9 Lessons for living longer from the people who've lived the longest. Washington, D.C.:

National Geographic.

Buettner, D., & Skemp, S. (2016). Blue zones. American Journal of Lifestyle Medicine, 10(5), 318–321. doi:10.1177/1559827616637066

Chang, A. M., Aeschbach, D., Duffy, J. F., & Czeisler, C. A. (2015). Evening use of light-emitting eReaders negatively affects sleep, circadian timing, and next-morning alertness. Proceedings of the National Academy of Sciences, 112(4), 1232-1237.

Choi, I. Y., Piccio, L., Childress, P., Bollman, B., Ghosh, A., Brandhorst, S., ... & Longo, V. D. (2019). A Diet Mimicking Fasting Promotes Regeneration and Reduces Autoimmunity and Multiple Sclerosis Symptoms. Cell Reports, 15(10), 2136-2146.

de Cabo, R., & Mattson, M. P. (2019). Effects of Intermittent Fasting on Health, Aging, and Disease. New England Journal of Medicine, 381(26), 2541-2551.

Dominguez, L. J., Veronese, N., & Barbagallo, M. (2024). The link between spirituality and longevity. Aging Clinical and Experimental Research, 36(1). doi:10.1007/s40520-023-02684-5

Drake, C., Roehrs, T., Shambroom, J., & Roth, T. (2013). Caffeine effects on sleep taken 0, 3, or 6 hours before going to bed.

Emmons, R. A., & McCullough, M. E. (2003). Counting blessings versus burdens: An experimental investigation of gratitude and subjective well-being in daily life. Journal of Personality and Social Psychology, 84(2), 377–389.

Epel, E. S., Blackburn, E. H., Lin, J., Dhabhar, F. S., Adler, N. E., Morrow, J. D., & Cawthon, R. M. (2009). Accelerated telomere shortening in response to life stress. Proceediangs of the National Academy of Sciences, 101(49), 17312-17315.

REFERENCE

Estruch, R., Ros, E., Salas-Salvadó, J., Covas, M. I., Corella, D., Arós, F., ... & Martínez-González, M. A. (2013). Primary prevention of cardiovascular disease with a Mediterranean diet supplemented with extra-virgin olive oil or nuts. New England Journal of Medicine, 368(14), 1279-1290.

Fredrickson, B. L., Cohn, M. A., Coffey, K. A., Pek, J., & Finkel, S. M. (2008). Open hearts build lives: Positive emotions, induced through loving-kindness meditation, build consequential personal resources. Journal of Personality and Social Psychology, 95(5), 1045-1062.

Goyal, M., Singh, S., Sibinga, E. M., Gould, N. F., Rowland-Seymour, A., Sharma, R., ... & Haythornthwaite, J. A. (2014). Meditation programs for psychological stress and well-being: A systematic review and meta-analysis. JAMA Internal Medicine, 174(3), 357–368.

Hartig, T., Mitchell, R., de Vries, S., & Frumkin, H. (2014). Nature and health. Annual Review of Public Health, 35, 207–228.

Henning, S. M., Yang, J., Shao, P., Lee, R. P., Huang, J., Ly, A., ... & Li, Z. (2017). Health benefit of vegetable/fruit juice-based diet: Role of microbiome. Scientific Reports, 7(1), 2167.

Herskind, A. M., McGue, M., Holm, N. V., Sørensen, T. I., Harvald, B., & Vaupel, J. W. (1996). The heritability of human longevity: A population-based study of 2872 Danish Twin Pairs born 1870–1900. Human Genetics, 97(3), 319–323. doi:10.1007/bf02185763

Johnston, W. M., & Davey, G. C. (1997). The psychological impact of negative TV news bulletins: The catastrophizing of personal worries. British Journal of Psychology, 88(Pt 1), 85–91.

Kanherkar, R. R., Bhatia-Dey, N., & Csoka, A. B. (2014). Epigenetics across the human lifespan. Frontiers in Cell and Developmental Biology, 2. doi:10.3389/fcell.2014.00049

Koenig, H. G. (2012). Religion, spirituality, and health: The research and clinical implications. *ISRN Psychiatry, 2012

Kumar, S., & Kaur, G. (2012). Intermittent fasting dietary restriction regimen negatively influences reproduction in young rats: A study of hypothalamo-hypophysial-gonadal axis. PLoS One, 7(3), e33468.

Levine, B., Packer, M., Codogno, P., & Kroemer, G. (2017). Development by Self-Digestion: Molecular Mechanisms and Biological Functions of Autophagy. Cell, 6(7), 463-477.

López-Otín, C., Blasco, M. A., Partridge, L., Serrano, M., & Kroemer, G. (2013). The hallmarks of aging. Cell, 153(6), 1194-1217.

Ma, X., Yue, Z. Q., Gong, Z. Q., Zhang, H., Duan, N. Y., Shi, Y. T., Wei, G. X., & Li, Y. F. (2017). The effect of diaphragmatic breathing on attention, negative affect and stress in healthy adults. Frontiers in Psychology, 8, 874.

Malshe, P. C. (2011). Nisshesha rechaka pranayama offers benefits through brief intermittent hypoxia. AYU, 32(4), 451-457.

Mattson, M. P., Longo, V. D., & Harvie, M. (2017). Impact of Intermittent Fasting on Health and Disease Processes. Ageing Research Reviews, 39, 46-58.

Pham-Huy, L. A., He, H., & Pham-Huy, C. (2008). Free radicals, antioxidants in disease and health. International journal of biomedical science : IJBS, 4(2), 89–96.

Rando, T. A., & Chang, H. Y. (2012). Aging, rejuvenation, and epigenetic reprogramming: resetting the aging clock. Cell, 148(1-2), 46-57.

Sharma, A., Madaan, V., & Petty, F. D. (2006). Exercise for mental health. Primary Care Companion to The Journal of Clinical Psychiatry, 8(2), 106.

Uchino, B. N. (2006). Social support and health: A review of physiological processes potentially underlying links to disease outcomes. Journal of Behavioral Medicine, 29(4), 377–387.

Varady, K. A., Bhutani, S., Church, E. C., & Klempel, M. C. (2013). Short-term modified alternate-day fasting: a novel dietary strategy for weight loss and cardioprotection in obese adults. The American Journal of Clinical Nutrition, 90(5), 1138-1143.

CHAPTER 2

American College of Sports Medicine. (2011). ACSM's guidelines for exercise testing and prescription. Lippincott Williams & Wilkins.

Anderson, E., & Shivakumar, G. (2013). Effects of exercise and physical activity on anxiety. Frontiers in Psychiatry, 4, 27.

Bjelakovic, G., Nikolova, D., Gluud, L. L., Simonetti, R. G., & Gluud, C. (2012). Antioxidant supplements for prevention of mortality in healthy participants and patients with various diseases. Cochrane Database of Systematic Reviews, (3).

Cappuccio, F. P., D'Elia, L., Strazzullo, P., & Miller, M. A. (2010). Sleep duration and all-cause mortality: a systematic review and meta-analysis of prospective studies. Sleep, 33(5), 585–592.

Casa, D. J., Armstrong, L. E., Hillman, S. K., Montain, S. J., Reiff, R. V., Rich, B. S., Roberts, W. O., & Stone, J. A. (2000). National Athletic Trainers' Association Position Statement: Fluid Replacement for Athletes. Journal of Athletic Training, 35(2), 212–224.

Colberg, S. R., Sigal, R. J., Fernhall, B., Regensteiner, J. G., Blissmer, B. J., Rubin, R. R., Chasan-Taber, L., Albright, A. L., & Braun, B. (2010). Exercise and Type 2 Diabetes: The American College of Sports Medicine and the American Diabetes Association: joint position statement. Diabetes Care, 33(12), e147-e167.

Garber, C. E., Blissmer, B., Deschenes, M. R., Franklin, B.

A., Lamonte, M. J., Lee, I. M., Nieman, D. C., & Swain, D. P. (2011). American College of Sports Medicine position stand. Quantity and quality of exercise for developing and maintaining cardiorespiratory, musculoskeletal, and neuromotor fitness in apparently healthy adults: Guidance for prescribing exercise. Medicine & Science in Sports & Exercise, 43(7), 1334-1359.

Gómez-Pinilla, F. (2008). Brain foods: the effects of nutrients on brain function. Nature Reviews Neuroscience, 9(7), 568–578.

Goyal, M., Singh, S., Sibinga, E. M., Gould, N. F., Rowland-Seymour, A., Sharma, R., ... & Haythornthwaite, J. A. (2014). Meditation programs for psychological stress and well-being: A systematic review and meta-analysis. JAMA Internal Medicine, 174(3), 357–368.

Holt-Lunstad, J., Smith, T. B., & Layton, J. B. (2010). Social relationships and mortality risk: a meta-analytic review. PLoS Medicine, 7(7), e1000316.

Hood, S., & Amir, S. (2017). The aging clock: circadian rhythms and later life. Journal of Clinical Investigation, 127(2), 437–446.

Janssen, I., & LeBlanc, A. G. (2010). Systematic review of the health benefits of physical activity and fitness in school-aged children and youth. International Journal of Behavioral Nutrition and Physical Activity, 7(1), 40.

Lee, I. M., & Skerrett, P. J. (2001). Physical activity and all-cause mortality: what is the dose-response relation? Journal of American Medicine, 285(11), 1447-1450.

Li, F., Harmer, P., Fitzgerald, K., Eckstrom, E., Stock, R., Galver, J., Maddalozzo, G., & Batya, S. S. (2012). Tai chi and postural stability in patients with Parkinson's disease. The New England Journal of Medicine, 366(6), 511-519.

Ludwig, D. S. (2011). Technology, diet, and the burden of chronic disease. JAMA, 305(13), 1352–1353.

McEwen, B. S. (2007). Physiology and Neurobiology of

Stress and Adaptation: Central Role of the Brain. Physiological Reviews, 87(3), 873–904.

Pandey, K. B., & Rizvi, S. I. (2009). Plant polyphenols as dietary antioxidants in human health and disease. Oxidative Medicine and Cellular Longevity, 2(5), 270–278.

Pham-Huy, L. A., He, H., & Pham-Huy, C. (2008). Free radicals, antioxidants in disease and health. International Journal of Biomedical Science : IJBS, 4(2), 89–96.

Popkin, B. M., D'Anci, K. E., & Rosenberg, I. H. (2010). Water, Hydration and Health. Nutrition Reviews, 68(8), 439–458. 9.

Ratini, M. (2023). Controlling stress: Causes of stress, reducing stress, and more. Retrieved from https://www.webmd.com/balance/all-stressed-out

Smyth, J. M., Zawadzki, M. J., Juth, V., & Sciamanna, C. N. (2018). Global Perceived Stress Predicts Cognitive Change Among Older Adults. Psychology and Aging, 33(4), 645–657.

Sutton, A. (2016). Measuring the effects of self-awareness: Construction of the self-awareness outcomes questionnaire. Europe's Journal of Psychology, 12(4), 645–658. doi:10.5964/ejop.v12i4.1178

Walker, M. P. (2017). Why We Sleep: Unlocking the Power of Sleep and Dreams. Scribner.

CHAPTER 3

Black, D. S., & Slavich, G. M. (2016). Mindfulness meditation and the immune system: A systematic review of randomized controlled trials. Annals of the New York Academy of Sciences, 1373(1), 13–24.

Burzler, M. A., Voracek, M., Hosner, R., & Stieger, S. (2019). A systematic review and meta-analysis of breathing techniques as a treatment for depression. Mindfulness, 10(2), 219–230.

Calogiuri, G., & Chroni, S. (2014). The impact of the natural environment on the promotion of active living: An integrative systematic review. BMC Public Health, 14, 873.

Condon, P., Desbordes, G., Miller, W. B., & DeSteno, D. (2013). Meditation increases compassionate responses to suffering. Psychological Science, 24(10), 2125–2127.

Coughlin, P. (2002). Principles and practice of Manual Therapeutics. New York: Churchill Livingstone.

Deutsch, J. E., & Anderson, E. Z. (2008). Complementary Therapies for Physical Therapy A Clinical Decision-Making Approach. Elsevier.

Emmons, R. A., & Mishra, A. (2011). Why gratitude enhances well-being: What we know, what we need to know. In K. M. Sheldon, T. B. Kashdan, & M. F. Steger (Eds.), Designing positive psychology: Taking stock and moving forward (pp. 248–262). Oxford University Press.

Farrar, A. J., & Farrar, F. C. (2020a). Clinical aromatherapy. Nursing Clinics of North America, 55(4), 489–504. doi:10.1016/j. cnur.2020.06.015

Fleming, S. A., & Gutknecht, N. C. (2010). Naturopathy and the Primary Care Practice. Primary Care: Clinics in Office Practice, 37(1), 119–136. doi:10.1016/j.pop.2009.09.002

Frank, D. L., Khorshid, L., Kiffer, J. F., McKee, M. G., & Moravec, C. S. (2010). Biofeedback in medicine: who, when, why and how? Mental Health in Family Medicine, 7(2), 85–91. doi:10.1016/j.ctcp.2022.101606

Goyal, M., Singh, S., Sibinga, E. M. S., Gould, N. F., Rowland-Seymour, A., Sharma, R., ... & Haythornthwaite, J. A. (2014). Meditation programs for psychological stress and well-being: A systematic review and meta-analysis. JAMA Internal Medicine, 174(3), 357–368.

Gowans, C. L., deHueck, A., Voss, S., & Silaj, A. (2019). Effect of a randomized, controlled trial of yoga on blood pressure in middle-aged and older adults. Hypertension Research, 42(4), 558-568.

Hanley, A. W., Lindahl, J. R., & Mehling, W. E. (2015). Mindful eating and living (MEAL): Weight, eating behavior, and psychological outcomes associated with a mindfulness-based intervention for people with obesity. Complementary Therapies in Medicine, 23(6), 767–774.

Jerath, R., Crawford, M. W., Barnes, V. A., & Harden, K. (2015). Self-regulation of breathing as a primary treatment for anxiety. Applied Psychophysiology and Biofeedback, 40(2), 107–115.

Johnson, D. B., & Lee, A. K. (2016). Physical activity's role in enhancing mental well-being and cognitive function. Journal of Physical Activity and Mental Health, 8(4), 456-468.

Jordan, C. H., Wang, W., Donatoni, L., & Meier, B. P. (2014). Mindful eating: Trait and state mindfulness predict healthier eating behavior. Personality and Individual Differences, 68, 107–111.

Kabat-Zinn, J. (2003). Mindfulness-based interventions in context: Past, present, and future. Clinical Psychology: Science and Practice, 10(2), 144–156.

Klein, A. V., & Kiat, H. (2014). Detox diets for toxin elimination and weight management: A Critical Review of the evidence. Journal of Human Nutrition and Dietetics, 28(6), 675–686. doi:10.1111/jhn.12286

Kondo, M. C., & Flaxman, S. (2018). Urban green space and its impact on human health. International Journal of Environmental Research and Public Health, 15(3), 445.

Liu, R. H. (2013). Health benefits of fruit and vegetables are from additive and synergistic combinations of phytochemicals. The American Journal of Clinical Nutrition, 78(3), 517S-520S.

Mackenzie, M. J., & Brymer, E. (2018). Conceptualizing adventurous nature sport: A positive psychology perspective. Annals of Leisure Research, 21(4), 407–424.

Matos, L. C., Machado, J. P., Monteiro, F. J., & Greten, H. J. (2021). Understanding traditional chinese medicine therapeutics: An overview of the basics and clinical applications. Healthcare, 9(3), 257. doi:10.3390/healthcare9030257

Mosunic, C. (2024). How (and why) to start a Gratitude Journal for your wellbeing. Retrieved from https://www.calm.com/blog/gratitude-journal

Oleson, T. (2014). Auriculotherapy Manual Chinese and Western Systems of ear acupuncture. Edinburgh: Churchill Livingstone Elsevier.

Rehman, T., & Ahmad , S. (2017). Introduction of homeopathy and homeopathic medicines: A review . International Journal of Homoeopathic Sciences, 1(3), 21–25.

Ross, A., & Thomas, S. (2010). The health benefits of yoga and exercise: a review of comparison studies. The Journal of Alternative and Complementary Medicine, 16(1), 3-12.

Smith, J. A., Doe, L. M., & White, R. S. (2016). The effects of diet rich in antioxidants on immune function and longevity. Journal of Health and Nutrition Research, 15(2), 123-135.

Tang, Y.-Y., Hölzel, B. K., & Posner, M. I. (2015). The neuroscience of mindfulness meditation. Nature Reviews Neuroscience, 16(4), 213–225.

Vickers, A. J., Vertosick, E. A., Lewith, G., MacPherson, H., Foster, N. E., Sherman, K. J., ... & Linde, K. (2018). Acupuncture for chronic pain: Update of an individual patient data meta-analysis. The Journal of Pain, 19(5), 455-474.

Warren, J. M., Smith, N., & Ashwell, M. (2017). A structured literature review on the role of mindfulness, mindful eating, and intuitive eating in changing eating behaviours: Effectiveness and associated potential mechanisms. Nutrition Research Reviews, 30(2), 272–283.

Watson, N. F., Badr, M. S., Belenky, G., Bliwise, D. L., Buxton, O. M., Buysse, D., ... & Tasali, E. (2018). Recommended Amount of Sleep for a Healthy Adult: A Joint Consensus Statement of the American Academy of Sleep Medicine and Sleep Research Society. Sleep, 38(6), 843-844.

Whatley, J., Perkins, J., & Samuel, C. (2022). 'reflexology: Exploring the mechanism of action.' Complementary Therapies in Clinical Practice, 48. doi:10.1016/j.ctcp.2022.101606

Willett, W., Rockström, J., Loken, B., Springmann, M., Lang, T., Vermeulen, S., ... & Murray, C. J. L. (2019). Food in the Anthropocene: the EAT–Lancet Commission on healthy diets from sustainable food systems. The Lancet, 393(10170), 447–492.

Woodyard, C. (2011). Exploring the therapeutic effects of yoga and its ability to increase quality of life. International Journal of Yoga, 4(2), 49–54. doi:10.4103/0973-6131.85485

https://www.ncbi.nlm.nih.gov/pmc/articles/PMC4940234/

https://journals.lww.com/psychosomaticmedicine/abstract/2021/07000/mindfulness_based_stress_reduction_buffers.16.aspx

CHAPTER 4

Antonucci, T. C., Ajrouch, K. J., & Birditt, K. S. (2014). The convoy model: Explaining social relations from a multidisciplinary perspective. The Gerontologist, 54(1), 82-92.

Chang, A.-M., Aeschbach, D., Duffy, J. F., & Czeisler, C. A. (2015). Evening use of light-emitting eReaders negatively affects sleep, circadian timing, and next-morning alertness. Proceedings of the National Academy of Sciences, 112(4), 1232-1237.

Diener, E., & Seligman, M. E. P. (2002). Very happy people. Psychological Science, 13(1), 81-84.

Holt-Lunstad, J., Smith, T. B., & Layton, J. B. (2010). Social relationships and mortality risk: A meta-analytic review. PLOS Medicine, 7(7), e1000316.

Piliavin, J. A., & Siegl, E. (2007). Health benefits of volunteering in the Wisconsin Longitudinal Study. Journal of Health and Social Behavior, 48(4), 450-464.

Post, S. G. (2005). Altruism, happiness, and health: It's good to be good. International Journal of Behavioral Medicine, 12(2), 66-77.

Primack, B. A., Shensa, A., Sidani, J. E., Whaite, E. O., yi Lin, L., Rosen, D., Colditz, J. B., Radovic, A., & Miller, E. (2017). Social media use and perceived social isolation among young adults in the U.S. American Journal of Preventive Medicine, 53(1), 1-8.

Starcevic, V., & Aboujaoude, E. (2017). Internet addiction: Reappraisal of an increasingly inadequate concept. CNS Spectrums, 22(1), 7-13.

Stebbins, R. A. (2007). Serious leisure: A perspective for our time. Transaction Publishers.

Turel, O., Serenko, A., & Giles, P. (2011). Integrating technology addiction and use: An empirical investigation of online auction users. MIS Quarterly, 35(4), 1043-1061.

Twenge, J. M., & Campbell, W. K. (2018). Associations between screen time and lower psychological well-being among children and adolescents: Evidence from a population-based study. Preventive Medicine Reports, 12, 271-283.

Williams, D. R., & Mohammed, S. A. (2009). Discrimination and racial disparities in health: Evidence and needed research. Journal of Behavioral Medicine, 32(1), 20-47.

CHAPTER 5

American Heart Association. (2024). American Heart Association recommendations for physical activity in adults and kids. Retrieved from https://www.heart.org/en/healthy-living/fitness/fitness-basics/aha-recs-for-physical-activity-in-adults

Anthonisen, N. R., Connett, J. E., Kiley, J. P., Altose, M. D., Bailey, W. C., Buist, A. S., ... & O'Hara, P. (1994). Effects of smoking intervention and the use of an inhaled anticholinergic bronchodilator on the rate of decline of FEV1. The Lung Health Study. JAMA, 272(19), 1497-1505.

Appel, L. J., Moore, T. J., Obarzanek, E., Vollmer, W. M., Svetkey, L. P., Sacks, F. M., ... & Cutler, J. A. (1997). A clinical trial of the effects of dietary patterns on blood pressure. DASH Collaborative Research Group. New England Journal of Medicine, 336(16), 1117-1124.

Bialystok, E., Craik, F. I., & Freedman, M. (2007). Bilingualism as a protection against the onset of symptoms of dementia. Neuropsychologia, 45(2), 459-464.

Boyle, S. H., Samad, Z., Becker, R. C., Williams, R., Kuhn, C., Ortel, T. L., ... & Blumenthal, J. A. (2017). The effects of mindfulness-based stress reduction on cardiac patients' blood pressure, perceived stress, and anger: A single-blind randomized controlled trial. Journal of Cardiopulmonary Rehabilitation and Prevention, 37(6), 370-377.

Christensen, R., Bartels, E. M., Astrup, A., & Bliddal, H. (2007). Effect of weight reduction in obese patients diagnosed with knee osteoarthritis: a systematic review and meta-analysis. Annals of the Rheumatic Diseases, 66(4), 433-439.

Cornelissen, V. A., & Smart, N. A. (2013). Exercise training for blood pressure: A systematic review and meta-analysis. Journal of the American Heart Association, 2(1), e004473.

Critchley, J. A., & Capewell, S. (2003). Mortality risk reduction associated with smoking cessation in patients with coronary heart disease: A systematic review. JAMA, 290(1), 86-97.

de Lorgeril, M., Salen, P., Martin, J. L., Monjaud, I., Delaye, J., & Mamelle, N. (1999). Mediterranean diet, traditional risk factors, and the rate of cardiovascular complications after myocardial infarction: Final report of the Lyon Diet Heart Study. Circulation, 99(6), 779-785.

Elmhurst, E. (2018). Has a serious or chronic illness got you depressed? Retrieved from https://www.eehealth.org/blog/2018/03/chronic-illness-depression/

Estruch, R., Ros, E., Salas-Salvadó, J., Covas, M. I., Corella, D., Arós, F., ... & Martínez-González, M. A. (2013). Primary prevention of cardiovascular disease with a Mediterranean diet supplemented with extra-virgin olive oil or nuts. New England Journal of Medicine, 368(14), 1279-1290.

Fiatarone, M. A., Marks, E. C., Ryan, N. D., Meredith, C. N., Lipsitz, L. A., & Evans, W. J. (1994). High-intensity strength training in nonagenarians. Effects on skeletal muscle. JAMA, 271(24), 3029-3034.

Geddes, E. L., Reid, W. D., Crowe, J., O'Brien, K., & Brooks, D. (2019). Inspiratory muscle training in adults with chronic obstructive pulmonary disease: An update of a systematic review. Respiratory Medicine, 103(12), 1705-1712.

Goyal, M., Singh, S., Sibinga, E. M., Gould, N. F., Rowland-Seymour, A., Sharma, R., ... & Haythornthwaite, J. A. (2014). Meditation programs for psychological stress and well-being: A systematic review and meta-analysis. JAMA Internal Medicine, 174(3), 357-368.

Hanson, C., Rutten, E. P., Wouters, E. F., & Rennard, S. (2013). Influence of diet and obesity on COPD development and outcomes. International Journal of Chronic Obstructive Pulmonary Disease, 9, 723-733.

REFERENCE

Hartmann, M., Kopf, S., Kircher, C., Faude-Lang, V., Djuric, Z., Augstein, F., ... & Herzog, W. (2012). Sustained effects of a mindfulness-based stress reduction intervention in individuals with type 2 diabetes: A randomized controlled trial. Psychotherapy and Psychosomatics, 81(5), 306-308.

Hawkley, L. C., & Cacioppo, J. T. (2010). Loneliness matters: A theoretical and empirical review of consequences and mechanisms. Annals of Behavioral Medicine, 40(2), 218-227.

He, F. J., & MacGregor, G. A. (2002). Effect of longer-term modest salt reduction on blood pressure. *Cochrane Database of Systematic Reviews, (1), CD004937.

Hertzog, C., Kramer, A. F., Wilson, R. S., & Lindenberger, U. (2009). Enrichment effects on adult cognitive development: Can the functional capacity of older adults be preserved and enhanced? Psychological Science in the Public Interest, 9(1), 1-65.

Hernández-Hernández, V., Ferraz-Amaro, I., & Díaz-González, F. (2014). Influence of exercise on patients with rheumatoid arthritis in the era of biologics. PM&R, 6(3), 275-282.

Hildon, Z., Smith, G., Netuveli, G., & Blane, D. (2008). Understanding adversity and resilience at older ages. Sociology of Health & Illness, 30(5), 726–740. doi:10.1111/j.1467-9566.2008.01087.x

Holt-Lunstad, J., Smith, T. B., & Layton, J. B. (2010). Social relationships and mortality risk: A meta-analytic review. PLOS Medicine, 7(7), e1000316.

Husain, K., Ansari, R. A., & Ferder, L. (2014). Alcohol-induced hypertension: Mechanism and prevention. Retrieved from https://www.ncbi.nlm.nih.gov/pmc/articles/PMC4038773/

Iqbal, A. M., & Jamal, S. F. (2023). Essential hypertension. Retrieved from https://www.ncbi.nlm.nih.gov/books/NBK539859/

Jacka, F. N., O'Neil, A., Opie, R., Itsiopoulos, C., Cotton, S., Mohebbi, M., ... & Castle, D. (2017). A randomised controlled trial of dietary improvement for adults with major depression (the 'SMILES' trial). BMC Medicine, 15(1), 23.

Jansen, M. J., Viechtbauer, W., Lenssen, A. F., Hendriks, E. J., & de Bie, R. A. (2011). Strength training alone, exercise therapy alone, and exercise therapy with passive manual mobilisation each reduce pain and disability in people with knee osteoarthritis: A systematic review. Journal of Physiotherapy, 57(1), 11-20.

Kable, J. W., Caulfield, M. K., Falcone, M., McConnell, M., Bernardo, L., Parthasarathi, T., ... & Lerman, C. (2017). No effect of commercial cognitive training on brain activity, choice behavior, or cognitive performance. Journal of Neuroscience, 37(31), 7390-7402.

Kim, B.-Y., Choi, D.-H., Jung, C.-H., Kang, S.-K., Mok, J.-O., & Kim, C.-H. (2017). Obesity and physical activity. Retrieved from https://www.ncbi.nlm.nih.gov/pmc/articles/PMC6484923/

Knowler, W. C., Barrett-Connor, E., Fowler, S. E., Hamman, R. F., Lachin, J. M., Walker, E. A., & Nathan, D. M. (2002). Reduction in the incidence of type 2 diabetes with lifestyle intervention or metformin. New England Journal of Medicine, 346(6), 393-403.

Knutson, K. L., & Van Cauter, E. (2008). Associations between sleep loss and increased risk of obesity and diabetes. Annals of the New York Academy of Sciences, 1129, 287-304.

Liu, C. J., & Latham, N. K. (2009). Progressive resistance strength training for improving physical function in older adults. *Cochrane Database of Systematic Reviews, (3), CD002759.

Look AHEAD Research Group. (2013). Cardiovascular effects of intensive lifestyle intervention in type 2 diabetes. New England Journal of Medicine, 369(2), 145-154.

Lopez, E. O., Ballard, B. D., & Jan, A. (2023). Cardiovascular disease. Retrieved from https://www.ncbi.nlm.nih.gov/books/NBK535419/

Luthar, S. S., Cicchetti, D., & Becker, B. (2000). The construct of resilience: A critical evaluation and guidelines for future work. Child Development, 71(3), 543-562.

National Institutes on Aging. (2020). Retrieved from https://www.nia.nih.gov/news/maintaining-mobility-and-preventing-disability-are-key-living-independently-we-age

National Institute of Mental Health. (2024c). Older adults and Mental Health. Retrieved from https://www.nimh.nih.gov/health/topics/older-adults-and-mental-health

Neter, J. E., Stam, B. E., Kok, F. J., Grobbee, D. E., & Geleijnse, J. M. (2003). Influence of weight reduction on blood pressure: A meta-analysis of randomized controlled trials. Hypertension, 42(5), 878-884.

Njoku, I. (2022). What is mental illness? Retrieved from https://www.psychiatry.org/patients-families/what-is-mental-illness

Nouchi, R., Taki, Y., Takeuchi, H., Hashizume, H., Akitsuki, Y., Shigemune, Y., ... & Kawashima, R. (2013). Brain training game boosts executive functions, working memory and processing speed in the young adults: A randomized controlled trial. PLoS One, 8(2), e55518.

Panuganti, K. K., Nguyen, M., & Kshirsagar, R. K. (2023). Obesity. Retrieved from https://www.ncbi.nlm.nih.gov/books/NBK459357/

Pendergast, T. (2023). Assistive Devices for Arthritis of the Hands: Protecting Your Joints. Retrieved from https://www.hss.edu/conditions_assistive-devices-for-the-hand-small-joint-protection.asp

Perlman, A. I., Sabina, A., Williams, A. L., Njike, V. Y., & Katz, D. L. (2006). Massage therapy for osteoarthritis of the knee: A randomized controlled trial. Archives of Internal Medicine,

166(22), 2533-2538.

Reid, M. C., Eccleston, C., & Pillemer, K. (2015). Management of chronic pain in older adults. BMJ, 350(feb13 2). doi:10.1136/bmj.h532

Sattelmair, J., Pertman, J., Ding, E. L., Kohl, H. W., Haskell, W., & Lee, I. M. (2011). Dose-response between physical activity and risk of coronary heart disease: A meta-analysis. Circulation, 124(7), 789-795.

Senthelal, S., Li, J., Ardeshirzadeh, S., & Thomas, M. A. (2023). Arthritis. Retrieved from https://www.ncbi.nlm.nih.gov/books/NBK518992/

Schuch, F. B., Vancampfort, D., Richards, J., Rosenbaum, S., Ward, P. B., & Stubbs, B. (2016). Exercise as a treatment for depression: A meta-analysis adjusting for publication bias. Journal of Psychiatric Research, 77, 42-51.

Siddharthan, T., Grigsby, M., Morgan, B., Kalyesubula, R., Wise, R. A., Kirenga, B., & Checkley, W. (2019). Prevalence of chronic respiratory disease in urban and rural Uganda. Retrieved from https://www.ncbi.nlm.nih.gov/pmc/articles/PMC6747035/

Sjösten, N. M., & Kivelä, S. L. (2006). The effects of physical exercise on depressive symptoms among the aged: A systematic review. International Journal of Geriatric Psychiatry, 21(5), 410-418.

Sköldstam, L., Brudin, L., Hagfors, L., & Johansson, G. (2003). Weight reduction is not a major reason for improvement in rheumatoid arthritis from lacto-vegetarian, vegan or Mediterranean diets. Nutrition Journal, 2, 15.

Snowden, D., Kemper, S., Mortimer, J. A., Greiner, L. H., Wekstein, D. R., & Markesbery, W. R. (2011). Linguistic ability in early life and cognitive function and Alzheimer's disease in late life. Findings from the Nun Study. JAMA, 275(7), 528-532.

Stahl, J. M., & Malhotra, S. (2023). Obesity Surgery Indications and contraindications. Retrieved from https://www.ncbi.nlm.nih.gov/books/NBK513285/

Umpierre, D., Ribeiro, P. A. B., Kramer, C. K., Leitão, C. B., Zucatti, A. T. N., Azevedo, M. J., ... & Schaan, B. D. (2011). Physical activity advice only or structured exercise training and association with HbA1c levels in type 2 diabetes: A systematic review and meta-analysis. JAMA, 305(17), 1790-1799.

Urwyler, P., Gupta, R. K., Falkner, M., Niklaus, J., Müri, R. M., & Nef, T. (2023). Tablet-based puzzle game intervention for cognitive function and well-being in healthy adults: Pilot feasibility randomized controlled trial. JMIR Aging, 6. doi:10.2196/46177

Uthman, O. A., van der Windt, D. A., Jordan, J. L., Dziedzic, K. S., Healey, E. L., Peat, G. M., & Foster, N. E. (2013). Exercise for lower limb osteoarthritis: systematic review incorporating trial sequential analysis and network meta-analysis. British Journal of Sports Medicine, 47(15), 984-988.

Vickers, A. J., Cronin, A. M., Maschino, A. C., Lewith, G., MacPherson, H., Foster, N. E., ... & Linde, K. (2012). Acupuncture for chronic pain: Individual patient data meta-analysis. Archives of Internal Medicine, 172(19), 1444-1453.

Wang, C., Schmid, C. H., Hibberd, P. L., Kalish, R., Roubenoff, R., Rones, R., & McAlindon, T. (2010). Tai chi is effective in treating knee osteoarthritis: A randomized controlled trial. Arthritis & Rheumatism, 62(11), 1545-1553.

Wang, Y., Lu, H., Li, S., Zhang, Y., Yan, F., Huang, Y., ... Ma, Y. (2022). Effect of cold and heat therapies on pain relief in patients with delayed onset muscle soreness: A network meta-analysis. Journal of Rehabilitation Medicine, 54. doi:10.2340/jrm.v53.331

Yusuf, S., Hawken, S., Ounpuu, S., Dans, T., Avezum, A., Lanas, F., ... & Lisheng, L. (2004). Effect of potentially modifiable risk factors associated with myocardial infarction in 52 countries (the INTERHEART study): case-control study. The Lancet, 364(9438), 937-952.

Zautra, A. J., Davis, M. C., Reich, J. W., Nicassario, P., Tennen, H., Finan, P., ... & Irwin, M. R. (2008). Comparison of cognitive behavioral and mindfulness meditation interventions on adaptation to rheumatoid arthritis for patients with and without a history of recurrent depression. Journal of Consulting and Clinical Psychology, 76(3), 408-421.

Zhao, R., Zhao, M., & Xu, Z. (2015). The effects of differing resistance training modes on the preservation of bone mineral density in postmenopausal women: A meta-analysis. Osteoporosis International, 26(5), 1605-1618.

CHAPTER 6

American Heart Association. (2020). American Heart Association Recommendations for Physical Activity in Adults and Kids. https://www.heart.org/en/healthy-living/fitness/fitness-basics/aha-recs-for-physical-activity-in-adults

Amin, S., Zhang, Y., Felson, D. T., Sawin, C. T., Hannan, M. T., Wilson, P. W., & Kiel, D. P. (2000). Estradiol, testosterone, and the risk for hip fractures in elderly men from the Framingham Study. The American Journal of Medicine, 108(9), 733-740.

Avis, N. E., Crawford, S. L., Greendale, G., Bromberger, J. T., Everson-Rose, S. A., Gold, E. B., ... & Kravitz, H. M. (2015). Duration of menopausal vasomotor symptoms over the menopause transition. JAMA Internal Medicine, 175(4), 531-539.

Baumgartner, R. N., Waters, D. L., Gallagher, D., Morley, J. E., & Garry, P. J. (1999). Predictors of skeletal muscle mass in elderly men and women. Mechanisms of Ageing and Development, 107(2), 123-136.

Bhattacharya, P., & Chatterjee, S. (2020). EFFECTS OF EXERCISE ON ANDROPAUSE: A FOCUSED REVIEW. International Journal for Innovative Research in Multidisciplinary Field, 29(1), 1–20.

REFERENCE

Boyle, P. A., Barnes, L. L., Buchman, A. S., & Bennett, D. A. (2009). Purpose in life is associated with mortality among community-dwelling older persons. Psychosomatic Medicine, 71(5), 574-579.

Colcombe, S., & Kramer, A. F. (2003). Fitness effects on the cognitive function of older adults: A meta-analytic study. Psychological Science, 14(2), 125-130.

Decaroli, M. C., & Rochira, V. (2017). Aging and sex hormones in males. Virulence, 8(5), 545-570.

El Khoudary, S. R., Aggarwal, B., Beckie, T. M., Hodis, H. N., Johnson, A. E., Langer, R. D., Limacher, M. C., Manson, J. E., Stefanick, M. L., & Allison, M. A. (2015). Menopause transition and cardiovascular disease risk: Implications for timing of early prevention: A scientific statement from the American Heart Association. Circulation, 132(21), 2039-2048.

Gitlin, L. N. (2003). Conducting research on home environments: Lessons learned and new directions. The Gerontologist, 43(5), 628-637.

Harman, S. M., Metter, E. J., Tobin, J. D., Pearson, J., & Blackman, M. R. (2001). Longitudinal effects of aging on serum total and free testosterone levels in healthy men. The Journal of Clinical Endocrinology & Metabolism, 86(2), 724-731.

Holt-Lunstad, J., Smith, T. B., & Layton, J. B. (2010). Social relationships and mortality risk: A meta-analytic review. PLOS Medicine, 7(7), e1000316. https://doi.org/10.1371/journal.pmed.1000316.

Lusardi, A., & Mitchell, O. S. (2007). Financial literacy and retirement preparedness: Evidence and implications for financial education. Business Economics, 42(1), 35-44.

Majumder, S., Mondal, T., & Deen, M. J. (2017). Wearable sensors for remote health monitoring. Sensors, 17(1), 130.

Martelli, M., Zingaretti, L., Salvio, G., Bracci, M., & Santarelli,

L. (2021). Influence of work on Andropause and Menopause: A systematic review. International Journal of Environmental Research and Public Health, 18(19), 10074. doi:10.3390/ijerph181910074

Moffat, S. D., Zonderman, A. B., Metter, E. J., Blackman, M. R., Harman, S. M., & Resnick, S. M. (2002). Free testosterone and risk for Alzheimer disease in older men. Neurology, 58(1), 118-121.

Rose, D., & Whelan, C. (2017). Menopause: Tips for managing mood swings. Retrieved from https://www.healthline.com/health/menopause-mood-swings

Rossouw, J. E., Anderson, G. L., Prentice, R. L., LaCroix, A. Z., Kooperberg, C., Stefanick, M. L., Jackson, R. D., Beresford, S. A., Howard, B. V., Johnson, K. C., ... & Wactawski-Wende, J. (2002). Risks and benefits of estrogen plus progestin in healthy postmenopausal women: Principal.

Rostami-Moez, M., Masoumi, S. Z., Otogara, M., Farahani, F., Alimohammadi, S., & Oshvandi, K. (2023). Examining the health-related needs of females during menopause: A systematic review study. Journal of Menopausal Medicine, 29(1), 1–20. doi:10.6118/jmm.22033

Santoro, N., Epperson, C. N., & Mathews, S. B. (2015). Menopausal symptoms and their management. Endocrinology and Metabolism Clinics of North America, 44(3), 497-515.

Sofi, F., Cesari, F., Abbate, R., Gensini, G. F., & Casini, A. (2010). Adherence to Mediterranean diet and health status: meta-analysis. BMJ, 341, c4229. https://doi.org/10.1136/bmj.c4229.

Sowers, M. F., Zheng, H., Tomey, K., Karvonen-Gutierrez, C., Jannausch, M., Li, X., Yosef, M., & Symons, J. (2006). Changes in bone resorption across the menopause transition: Effects of reproductive hormones, body size, and ethnicity. The Journal of Clinical Endocrinology & Metabolism, 91(7), 2774-2782.

Wister, A. V., Coatta, K. L., Schuurman, N., Lear, S. A., Rosin, M., & MacKey, D. (2016). A lifecourse model of multimorbidity resilience: Theoretical and research developments. The Journal of Aging Studies, 38, 1-12.

Yardley, J. E., Sigal, R. J., Kenny, G. P., Riddell, M. C., Lovblom, L. E., & Perkins, B. A. (2016). Point-of-care HbA1C level and risk of diabetes-related complications. Journal of Diabetes and its Complications, 30(2), 210-216.

CHAPTER 7

Altini, M., & Plews, D. (2021). What is behind changes in resting heart rate and heart rate variability? A large-scale analysis of longitudinal measurements acquired in free-living. Sensors, 21(23), 7932. doi:10.3390/s21237932

Armanios, M., & Blackburn, E. H. (2012). The telomere syndromes. Nature Reviews Genetics, 13(10), 693-704.

Artandi, S. E., & DePinho, R. A. (2010). Telomeres and telomerase in cancer. Carcinogenesis, 31(1), 9-18.

Aviv, A., Hunt, S. C., Lin, J., Cao, X., Kimura, M., & Blackburn, E. (2011). Impartial comparative analysis of measurement of leukocyte telomere length/DNA content by Southern blots and qPCR. Nucleic Acids Research, 39(20), e134.

Bernardes de Jesus, B., & Blasco, M. A. (2016). The potential of telomerase activation in extending health span and longevity. Current Opinion in Cell Biology, 40, 126-133.

Blackburn, E. H., Epel, E. S., & Lin, J. (2015). Human telomere biology: A contributory and interactive factor in aging, disease risks, and protection. Science, 350(6265), 1193-1198.

Bravata, D. M., Smith-Spangler, C., Sundaram, V., Gienger, A. L., Lin, N., Lewis, R., ... & Sirard, J. R. (2007). Using pedometers to increase physical activity and improve health: A systematic review. JAMA, 298(19), 2296-2304.

Bussian, T. J., et al. (2018). Clearance of senescent glial cells prevents tau-dependent pathology and cognitive decline. Nature, 562, 578-582.

Cawthon, R. M., Smith, K. R., O'Brien, E., Sivatchenko, A., & Kerber, R. A. (2003). Association between telomere length in blood and mortality in people aged 60 years or older. The Lancet, 361(9355), 393-395.

Childs, B. G., et al. (2017). Senescence and senolytics: Therapeutic implications for chronic diseases of aging. Biochemical Pharmacology, 136, 139-150.

Chinoy, E. D., Cuellar, J. A., Huwa, K. E., James, K. A., Hirsch, A. G., VoPham, T., ... & Plaku-Alakbarova, B. (2021). Sleep disorder diagnosis and treatment during the COVID-19 pandemic: A systematic review. Sleep Medicine Reviews, 60, 101556.

Crous-Bou, M., Fung, T. T., Prescott, J., Julin, B., Du, M., Sun, Q., Rexrode, K. M., Hu, F. B., & De Vivo, I. (2014). Mediterranean diet and telomere length in Nurses' Health Study: population based cohort study. BMJ, 349, g6674.

De Jesus, B. B., Schneeberger, K., Vera, E., Tejera, A., Harley, C. B., & Blasco, M. A. (2011). The telomerase activator TA-65 elongates short telomeres and increases health span of adult/ old mice without increasing cancer incidence. Aging Cell, 10(4), 604-621.

Epel, E. S., Blackburn, E. H., Lin, J., Dhabhar, F. S., Adler, N. E., Morrow, J. D., & Cawthon, R. M. (2004). Accelerated telomere shortening in response to life stress. Proceedings of the National Academy of Sciences, 101(49), 17312-17315.

Franco, R. Z., Fallaize, R., Lovegrove, J. A., & Hwang, F. (2016). Popular nutrition-related mobile apps: A feature assessment. JMIR mHealth and uHealth, 4(3), e85.

German, J. B., Zivkovic, A. M., Dallas, D. C., & Smilowitz, J. T.

REFERENCE

(2011). Nutrigenomics and personalized diets: What will they mean for food? Annual Review of Food Science and Technology, 2(1), 97–123. doi:10.1146/annurev.food.102308.124147

Heather, J. M., & Chain, B. (2016). The sequence of sequencers: The history of sequencing DNA. Genomics, 107(1), 1–8. doi:10.1016/j.ygeno.2015.11.003

Hernandez, L. M., & Blazer, D. G. (2006). Genes, behavior, and the Social Environment: Moving Beyond the Nature/nurture debate. Washington, DC.: National academic Press.

Justice, J. N., et al. (2019). Senolytics in idiopathic pulmonary fibrosis: Results from a first-in-human, open-label, pilot study. EBioMedicine, 40, 554-563.

Justice, J. N., Nambiar, A., Tchkonia, T., LeBrasseur, N. K., Pascual, R., Hashmi, S. K., ... & Kirkland, J. L. (2018). Senolytics in idiopathic pulmonary fibrosis: Results from a first-in-human, open-label, pilot study. *

Kirkland, J. L., & Tchkonia, T. (2017). Cellular senescence: A translational perspective. EBioMedicine, 21, 21-28.

Lorenzo, E. C., Torrance, B. L., & Haynes, L. (2023). Impact of senolytic treatment on immunity, aging, and disease. Frontiers in Aging, 4. doi:10.3389/fragi.2023.1161799

Matthews, C. E., Moore, S. C., Sampson, J., Blair, A., Xiao, Q., Keadle, S. K., Hollenbeck, A., & Park, Y. (2017). Mortality benefits for replacing sitting time with different physical activities. Medicine & Science in Sports & Exercise, 49(9), 1809-1816.

Piwek, L., Ellis, D. A., Andrews, S., & Joinson, A. (2016). The rise of consumer health wearables: Promises and barriers. PLOS Medicine, 13(2), e1001953.

Shammas, M. A. (2011). Telomeres, lifestyle, cancer, and aging. Current Opinion in Clinical Nutrition and Metabolic Care, 14(1), 28–34. doi:10.1097/mco.0b013e32834121b1

Shay, J. W., & Wright, W. E. (2000). Hayflick, his limit, and cellular ageing. Nature Reviews Molecular Cell Biology, 1(1), 72-76.

Tchkonia, T., et al. (2013). Cellular senescence and the senescent secretory phenotype: therapeutic opportunities. The Journal of Clinical Investigation, 123(3), 966-972.

Torkamani, A., Wineinger, N. E., & Topol, E. J. (2018). The personal and clinical utility of polygenic risk scores. Nature Reviews Genetics, 19(9), 581-590.

Xu, M., et al. (2018). Senolytics improve physical function and increase lifespan in old age. Nature Medicine, 24(8), 1246–1256.

Zhu, Y., Tchkonia, T., Pirtskhalava, T., Gower, A. C., Ding, H., Giorgadze, N., ... & Kirkland, J. L. (2017). The Achilles' heel of senescent cells: From transcriptome to senolytic drugs. Aging Cell, 16(3), 547-550.